flowers of ice

Donated to
SAINT PAUL PUBLIC LIBRARY

flowers of ice

IMANTS ZIEDONIS

Translated by BARRY CALLAGHAN

Preface by JOHN MONTAGUE

The Sheep Meadow Press
RIVERDALE-ON-HUDSON, NEW YORK

Copyright © 1987 by Imants Ziedonis

Copyright © 1987 by Exile Editions Limited

All rights reserved.

First published in Canada by Exile Editions Limited in 1987.

First published in the United States by the Sheep Meadow Press in 1990.

All inquiries and permission requests should be addressed to:
The Sheep Meadow Press, P.O. Box 1345,
Riverdale-on-Hudson, New York 10471.

Distributed by Consortium Book Sales & Distribution, Inc.
213 East 4th Street
St. Paul, MN 55101

Typeset in PALATINO *by* CAPS & LOWER CASE
Designed by LOU LUCIANI

ISBN 0-935296-89-1

Many people have aided me in translating
and understanding the poems of Imants Ziedonis.
I would like to thank, in particular, Baiba
and Baņuta Rubess, and
Vaira Vīķe-Freiberga to whom
I am also indebted for the insights gained
in the Latvian *daina* tradition and ancient
Latvian mythology.
Vilis Vitols provided the initiative and major
assistance for the project.

B.C.

This book is published by the Sheep Meadow Press,
Riverdale-on-Hudson, New York 10471

*This translation is for
Baiba Rubess
who introduced me to
the Ziedonis poems*

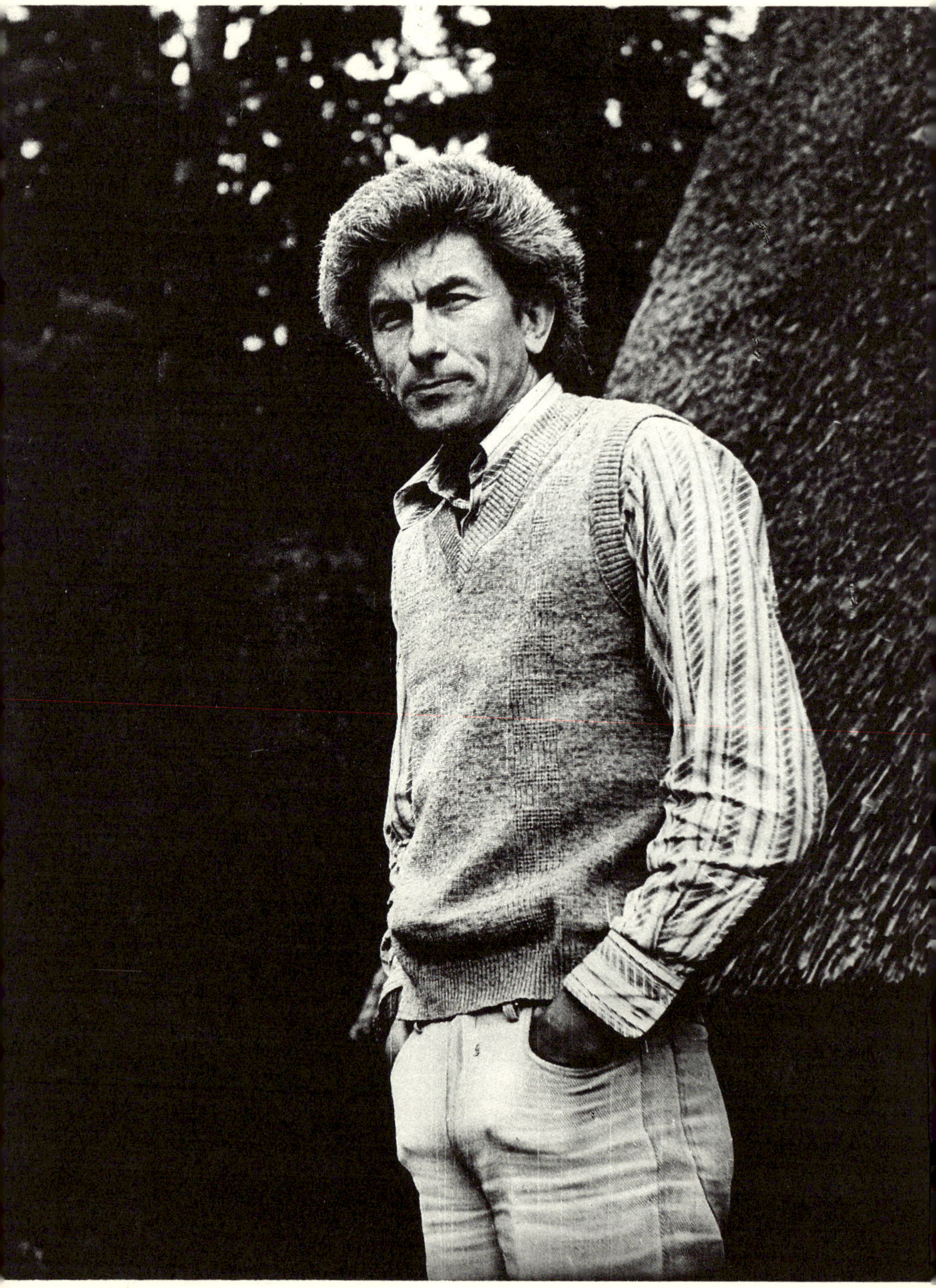

Preface

Forefathers and family
    my taproot…

There are major themes of our time which are also timeless. Like the plight of subject peoples: the smaller you are, the harder it is. The Moghuls poured over Northern India for centuries: some mingled with the native population, others used them, but most were absorbed into the great stockpot of India. There are always invaders, newcomers, strangers: Teutonic knights, Viking berserkers, clanking Normans in their shirts of mail. Some settle down:

> Every day I greet the passing
> axe children,
> who wax tall with my own small children.

Hence the problem of preserving the older traditions, at home and overseas, is a permanent one:

> O, Lord, they rooted the linden out of my land.
> Uprooted the linden tree –
> and dibbled her down –
> O Lord, down beyond the sea.

Sometimes the nation overseas, Sikhs in Canada, St. Patrick's Day Irish everywhere, White Russians in Paris, are more furious in their faith than the mother land. But there must be both:

> True, there must be
> that far tree –
> but nearby –
> we need one nearby, too!

"Tree" seems to me a central modern poem on the uprooting of peoples. Then there is the countryside, the earth herself. People prefer to ignore it but we have lived through an Agricultural Revolution as drastic as anything since the

Enclosure Acts, which inspired Goldsmith's greaty outcry, *The Deserted Village*. Common Market Agricultural Policy or collectivization, the result is the same; "rural mirth and manners are no more." One cannot read "By the Roadside" without mourning for that lost life, before the mechanical mastodons crunched down hedges and houses. Like Goldsmith, the mood of Ziedonis is one of pained nostalgia, this side of the sentimental:

> There were households here.
> Ashes turn to blossoms,
> bricks take root in the grass, pain
> in plots of remembrance.

This centralizing process is also connected with the wiping out of superstition, otherwise known as earth wisdom. A Nobel laureate whose origins are in the same area, Milosz, confesses to being haunted by a childish crime, the killing of a snake. Why is explained in "At Maruža's" where the milk suckling serpent nourishes the women and children. The simplicity of this rite affronts the Christianizing invader; when the Welshman, Giraldus Cambrensis, wrote that the Irish copulated with horses he was preparing the overthrow of the cult of Epona, the Celtic horse goddess. Soon the Normans clanked ashore with a papal bull to cleanse the Irish "abominations and vices" just as Germans, from Bremen, came to Latvia complaining:

> This non-German people is still in
> thrall to false Gods;
> they pray to the sun,
> moon, stars, fire, water...

Then there is song which preserves the bond between an ancient people and their past, so "never sup as song is sung, child!" In Gaelic, the old poetry went underground, to flow again as folksong. The reverse seems to have happened in Latvian, where poetry found roots in folksong; the work of

Ziedonis has a rich lyric base. And both traditions developed an elaborate frame of reference, a sort of double writing, a politic shorthand. So the country becomes a series of synonyms, the Wandering Heifer in Irish, the Mother of Cows in Latvian, potent symbols for a pastoral world resisting change induced by powerful neighbors. For the heritage is always menaced:

> Mother dear, you may draw pure milk from the teat
> but the song your daughter sings is watered down.

So the Muse in Ziedonis appears as a warm countrywoman, smelling of apples and milk, "Open as a golden door." Annele is one of her code names and she has a two-way teasing relationship with her poet. "You've missed the point again," she says, or more sharply, "Aren't you writing poems any more?" But the feminine is always a source:

> What kind of song is that, my sweet? I didn't know
> then, or now. It must be mine
> but it's likely hers.

Above all, although the poetry of Ziedonis has deep roots in soil, song and family secrets, it has a completely modern tone; the poem is extended in an extraordinary way by Ziedonis in his "Epiphanies", reminiscent of Eastern European poets like Herbert and Holub. Who else would compare the tension between the soul and God to a game of soccer? Above all, this poet is for the grain of the real. Woodshavings bring memories of grandfather's coffin but also a paean of hatred for that typical modern substitute:

> Chipboard is all the current rage. What a violation,
> vicious. Imagine the chips of a tree lying down beside
> chips from another tree in a presswood sheet, alien pulp,
> cemented by synthetic glue in some press, this glue the
> only bond that binds, nothing else. Like a couple at
> cross-purposes, or friends who've calculated their affairs.

A defender of all that is growing and natural, the poet dreams the revenge of nature on the city in "The Green Fairy Tale." One of the oldest of literary forms becomes a modern parable, a haunting possibility, a frightening glimpse of all we have lost, a surrealist warning to sober us all:

> Every year the green forest comes to the city and kills off the stench and reek of the city, silences the noises, destroys dust ... When it left, I felt so sad – I wanted to go with it. It'll come again this year. But no one knows when. I was in the forest yesterday. I listened, looked – not a sign. I asked, "Won't you come to the city? Won't you?" Silence.

JOHN MONTAGUE

flowers of ice

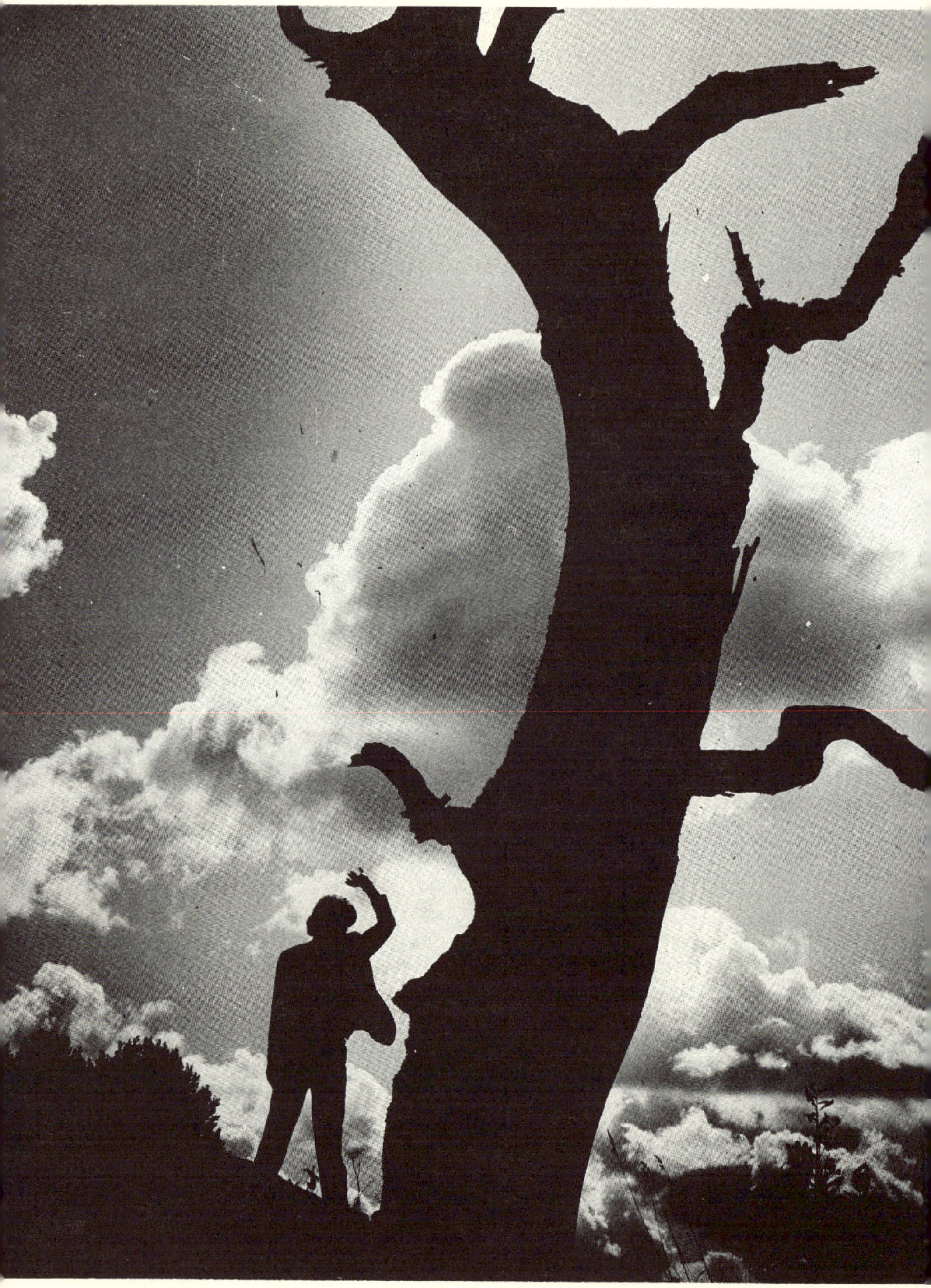

Epiphany 1

...Skirt a flower or the sea. It's all the same. A flower swells like the sea. But don't rush headlong into the sea, don't wade into a flower, don't step into someone's soul – stay close, shadow, enclose.

The noon hour sea is full of light, the sky's gift. At night the sea is heavy with heat, the day's gift. Of a summer night, I stroll the shore: it exudes warmth. I keep to the edge with my arms spread like wings, one in midnight mist, clinging to the land, the other seaborne. I call that intimacy. This is it.

I walk by the sea on windy nights. Waves spilling out of the sea's darkness, shoals of sound I still cannot see. Then the sudden roar of water on a sandbank, a white lip, a row of laughing teeth...dims, again it's dark. No shore, no distance, only a depthless darkness, seam on seam of white surf, a brief rustle and sheen. A row of white teeth.

Nearness of the sea.

Have you sought a haystack in a night meadow? A hayrick? Go into the dark meadow, widen your arms and listen for the well of heat. A stutter-step or two, and as if caught in a childhood game of treasure trove, someone says:

– Warm...warmer...hot...

You reach to the left, heat, large like a haystack. Before easing into this heat I skirt the stack, its invisible border, its sacred nimbus – the rim where the hay's radiance ends.

A cook circles the tureen, rims the plate. Food's not only a brimming bowl or a spoon in a greedy mouth, but a banked aroma above the bowl, tiny aromas typhooning in kitchen skies.

Sometimes it's unsettling heading straight into a strange house. Like cracking open a barely understood soul. So I scout around the house. Each house has its radiance, its possible aura. Some have only a small wreath of radiation around a window or door. With other houses, it flows on fences, slinks down lanes, beckoning you from kilometres away.

I circle the invisible borderline, the enclosed intimacy of the house.

A household that has bees radiates in the distance. It radiates down the by-ways of bees. Places of intense radiance. Widespread, benevolent radiance. Places I'd bring children to for their noonday nap.

Beeless houses shed less radiance. Still, getting closer, you hear the clucking of a hen who's laid an egg. I pay close attention, understand her completely: she cannot contain herself, her pride – since the egg really is fresh and brown with tiny dark speckles, and the yolk inside is bright as an orange.

But still I shun the house – heading into the woodshed instead, where woodland radiance holds court, but the trees' last lament is in sacrificial chimney smoke, scent of wood shavings.

Closeness of thrushes to the birch, the closeness of storks to the oak, eaves and swallows, and peonies beneath the window sill. So too, the house feels close, and I enter.

The child still unborn, but close.
You're close and soon I'll see you.
Enclosing.
Closing in.
Close.

Epiphany II

Never sup as song is sung, child! Never sup as song is sung, sweet child! A starveling slip of a soul may be inside the song mewling at this moment. Never sup as song is sung, child.

Never sip as song is sung, child! The oriole sings pleading for rain, or perhaps a drop of dew on leaves. The pleading oriole, parched and unfed, sings.

Child, we're a nation at sup, but set spoon in bowl as song is sung, sweet child. Turn away, child, as nuncle sups, and take no heed. He's swallowed all his songs, cannot separate songs from salad.

Spoon and song share one door. Will spoon pause at the mouth as song appears singing? Child, seize spoon by the hand, lead her aside, let song pass, O sweet child mine...

At Maruža's

In a shack of trimmed fir struts and a mud floor
trampled solid, a large clay tureen was buried
to the lip in the middle of the floor.
Not many came by here, but down the road a piece –
houses and clearings, and well-worked fields.

Ruža blended her herbal brew here.

Once upon a time, a grim German monk with cross and bible
stumbled into this calm wooded corner
and saw serpents suckling a cow.
The monk blessed himself, cut a hefty branch,
and slew the biggest snake.

So it goes. But no one knew why
Ruža was so suddenly aware.
Horrified, she leapt through the shack door
and began loud wailing:
"O Milk-Mother, my Milk-Mother!"
Coiled and beautiful, with golden ears,
milk leaking from the huge serpent,
seeping into the mouldering, stumpy earth.

And suddenly there was also wailing
in all the houses: "O murdered, O my Milk-Mother!"

As with church bells in later years,
women called through the woods
and in the clustered houses of almost every clan
there was always a woman protecting serpents.

And the lamenting assembled at Ruža's
and cast green grass over the serpent
and wept in the green weeds.

So it was done, Maruža told me.
Ruža didn't own a cow,
but she knew some milk spells –
and when she clapped her knife-handle against
a crock, serpents and toads lugged
themselves from caves, out from under
the thresholds of huts,
and spewed white milk suckled from cows
into the tureen in the middle of the floor.
Ruža always had enough milk.

But the monk reported to holy Rome:

> ...The first Litvaks I met worshipped (tended) snakes, and every head of a household kept a snake in a corner which he fed and, while she slept in the hay, brought her sacrifice.

And the monks learned much more: how to launch
toads into the air from a slab of see-saw wood,
a toad at one end, a big stone dropped,
catapulting the little creature, who plummets
and splatters, soaking the earth with milk.
And wrote to Rome:

> ...This non-German people is still in thrall to false gods; they pray to the sun, moon, stars, fire, water, the river, believing garter snakes and evil toads are gods; which, as I myself have to some extent seen, were fat and swollen. After they've been thrown or battered, they burst their bodies leaking bountiful milk.

And during the war, German officers fed at our table, swilled our milk, and stuffed like pigs, undid their belt buckles and passed foul wind; we all felt ashamed, since for children this was forbidden, but apparently among them it's quite common. Probably knights also farted at table, maybe monks as well.

And wrote to Rome:

> The garter snakes were so tame and lethargic that...even their children played with them...They slept in the children's cradles and supped with children from the same bowl.

Some incomprehensible code of cleanliness sent them into a rage. First they murdered the serpents and sawed down sacrificial linden trees, then they began to burn witches. But the secret stayed secret. And they wrote to Rome:

> ...It is clearly known, toads and snakes suckle cows, but what baffling art allows them to beguile on demand suckled milk into saucers, and hand it down, regained, retained...

Mother's The Essence

Mother's the essence of this poem.
The babe begins with milk
and aged returns to the teat to milk
more life from time – that's how it is.

Behold – it's wise to speak of milk.
Whatever's happening: lack of milk is the problem.

War and murder broke out
after the earth ran out of milk.
Mother couldn't suckle her son forever.
So he ambled off to find food for himself.
Never any good at seeding and tending drills,
and more cunning than other animals,
he ate his fill of what he killed.

In time, he killed time – by killing.

With a thousand elk on the island,
and ten thousand brothers mine,
and ten thousand brothers his,
would all brothers have enough elk?

So the king decided we'd run of out of elk,
and to call for a culling of the clans, or fratricide.
But their brothers didn't want to die.
So war broke out. Stoked by meat.

Stooped with age, the blood shed,
his face scarred, a greying soldier
came home to mother sporting medals on his chest
and with the war over the medic
recommended drinking fresh milk, a diet of honey.

A greying soldier came home to mother
for milk.

But mother had no medals, no renown.
All her life she'd gathered sweet grass
for the cow, sedge on the heath,
and now she set a wedge of homemade cheese on the table,
and cream, and freshly churned butter
and said: – Eat! In the fall there'll be a calf –

The son took all this in stride, his due.
He'd kept his mother's cow
from killers by killing another clan's
hundred thousand cows.
But mother? The witless woman cried:
– My, it's good you're home. You shouldn't be out there killing.

Mother was in her dotage, a little slow.
Plod and boredom had narrowed
the margins of her mind.
She cooed to the cows outside the cattle shed,
and the sorrel by the roadside, and the dogs,
and put snowdrops in the old vase.

Still her boy was due his soldier's dollop of butter.

This Morning

This morning I saw
a nightingale.
Songless
in the linden
still as spilt water.

Night fell like rain
through a drawn seine,
and an evening dew
unborn anew.

Trio

The wryneck chirps
Fourteen clockwork chimes.
Lindens break into bloom.

Milkweed flowers, oaks bud and
fir trees fuse the first green fist.
A pelting rain of yellow pollen.

Undīne says even nettles are sprouting.
What a boon.
She'll bestow
blossoms
on Ilmārs, that buffoon.

Krišjānis Peters Was Just Born

Born. A birth in time saves nine. Born, in the nick of time, before the solstice fern blossomed. The corncrake called and flames whirled in the tar barrel and tar trailed through green grass.

Suddenly someone screamed and we all wheeled as was our wont, each anticipating annunciation, one on a white horse, or one on a hedgehog in a bristling coat: the world was alive tonight: bubbles in the mug moaned, full throated frogs with puffed gills sang under a cover of lush green.

The girls' garters squealed and woollen yarn squealed, but it was dark and no one understood the colors of their cry.

Now, you knew someone's time was upon us.

Then stump screamed in the fire and a tongue shot out of the mouth, wanting to say a word, still unaware of what the word was.

Someone came along the gravel seashore, and a seagull rose from a rock, shaken from night sleep; I cast an eye after her but she was gone; we caroused and carried on.

But the rose riven at its root uttered a moan, and water in the well cried. Somebody stood up, said he's very thirsty.

We did not wander far from the fire, only to the rim of firelight. Because we'd been promised.

A coming. To dwell among us. And break bread among us. And cram us together, even closer.

And the tip of the fire is like the tip of the fir tree, only livelier, and so she writhes; windless, all alone.

Someone cast a beer mug onto the coals, someone a slice of cheese, and, as if responding to a primal urge, we began to cast sacrifices onto the embers, something fine from each of us. Whatever; a hat, a hair-pin, knife, glasses, powder compact. I threw into the fire a handkerchief full of ant alcohol soaked up from an ant hill.

And Jānis cast a gold ring onto the coals, and a voice within the fire said: you'll reap what you sow.

So, a son was born to Jānis. We saw not, but it is said he is born among us, Krišjānis by name.

Born among us at the appropriate hour. He will dwell among us.

He came propitiously, a solstice child. He will carouse in sunrises. All children born on Pēteris' day and Miķelis' day will be close by. No further than a seed flies.

Tree

Being a dog –
you need a tree to lift your leg;
comes the flood –
you need a sliver to keep afloat.

It's time I
turned the sod and shod myself in time – moil the earth;
and bury roots
in the ditched soil.

As I shelter
by the apple tree petals fall,
fall from the apple bough,
white petals fall, my salt tears fall, fall.

Every day I greet the passing
axe children,
children of the axe
who wax tall with my own small children.

I rooted the linden in –
O, Lord, I dibbled her down in the middle of the yard! –
and the linden sprang to the air.
– O, Lord, Lāčplēsis sprang from the linden and Koknesis'
nine sons fair.

Rooted the linden out –
O, Lord, they rooted the linden out of my land.
Uprooted the linden tree –
and dibbled her down –
O Lord, down beyond the sea.

Beyond the sea –
let it be – let nine boughs be, and bloom across the sea for
    Ieviņa, too!
And yet,
when white apple petals fall,

I say:
ease the spade into the earth here, dig it right here
to hitch the horse, hitch
the homestead and hitch landhome.

Whitsuntide,
when birch trees wither, are cut into kindling – who
cons a root,
or considers roots! O – our stripling daughters.

And if floods
come, who'll have a sliver, or a mooring slip
for a boat?
Or shade from the sun for the wayfarer laying out
his daily bread.

Dibble a tree,
it breaks the light, tree broken by hanged men, by fruit –
O yes, where there are trees
someone always breaks, and breaks.

But dibble in anyway.
Dibble the root! Plants are falling stars
whose earthbound tails
feed faith, legends, history.

Morning in
and morning out the sun rises in a red willow;
young lords in
are old lords out in search of that sapling.

True, there must be
that far tree –
but nearby –
we need one nearby, too!

As my lord leaps
from his horse he'll have no hitching tree –
dwarf pines,
a bush garden!

O lord, O lord
as I totter from the tavern,
if only there were a single
tree, one small tree to hold onto!

The Topmost Twig

There's no doubt,
the topmost twig is free.
Treetops only seem
to run in circles.

A honed simplicity:
three hundred and eight branches
three million bristling needles
ride the wind.

The Needle

Truly, if we are the needle,
children are the point.
But the old are the needle's eye,
thread drawn through them.

Why the devil do we darn the world,
why the devil do we puncture such a fine world
if thread isn't drawn
through grandmother!

The Chain

Truly, a chain has at least three links.
Even then – what'll you tether with something so short?

But father's watch chain had been in the family for years.
After the flood of front lines across the land
it was spirited away into the world.
Somewhere on the road among strangers
it's probably occupied
with pure Latvian.

Jānis, the neighbor, is charmed, –
Somehow nothing was ever
stolen from his father.

Grandmother

Grandmother?
Grandmother's a thumb.
We cannot put a plate on the table
or wash dishes
minus a thumb.

We cannot hold a cup
and drain it down
minus a thumb.
We cannot hold a pair of shears
or scissor a bridal veil
or shroud
minus a thumb.

Grandfather is also a thumb.
Where will you climb, my boy, minus a thumb?
What'll you do with an axe, my boy – minus a thumb?
How will you ever thumb your nose, my boy?

Families

Families are lean boats in eternity's lagoons;
a single life is a mere scull.
With only one or two generations in tow, –
now he's here, now he drowns.

Families are skis ferrying kin
across endless snows of being and non-.
Fleshed out fully to three (or four) generations,
we won't bog down, or drown.

The leaner the arrow, the likelier
a shot into eternity will home in on target.
An arrow, ripe with generations, will split that space
undeflected.
In the boundless ether of ebb and flux,
becoming, dissolution, and the drift of grazing dust –
forefathers and family
my taproot.

My Son, My Son

I tumbled onto the barrow
and arose joint by joint, –
the soil numbered me
among sons.

I fumbled around on the barrow
wearing a rasping workshirt, –
The soil embraced me
as a brother in sadness.

Given a white shirt,
a clean white shirt,
I dibbled and baled –
and was anointed a man.

Fog and dew, fog and dew
gave me my middle years –
now I am a father
given fatherhood.

My son, my son:
choose!
What are you doing here
tumbled onto the barrow?

Spring

Spring, you see, has sprung, the linden's
    in full flower
and Alīna glowers beside the tree in dung-crusted
    gumboots and weeps.
I can't comfort her: beauty, her presence,
    is pitiless.

Sister, I Unveil

> *Sunday morning herding cattle*
> *I wound fog into a ball*
> *whenever I see strangers*
> *I weave myself into a fog*
> **FOLK SONG**

Sister, I unveil
my soul to you
my pure soul
so secret

Brother, I bequeath
unto you my eyes
shutter them from
the bleaching sun

Daddystrange
because my hand is hot,
hot, my hand –
the clasp must be cold

the white pine sheathed with bark
the birch sheathed with white bark
the soul swathed
itself in white white mist

Purity

As Alina scours the milk pans
it crosses my mind that
she's pure white too.

Strawberry blooms are white
and in our marsh – meadowrue,
and a marvellous fruit
the snow apple,
 — around here, you're hard put to handle a grimy towel.

A Faith In Me

Sisters sprawled on furs, brothers sucking bones,
A dark absence settles over the hills
A core of distant loneliness so hollow
I long for someone to trust.

My tousled head of hair – lies in your lap:
Joy, or the jugular? – I couldn't care less,
The reek of meadow grass and nightshade
Makes my skin crawl.

Insane! Yes – and primitive! But cupped hands
Enclose a crystal sound – unlike the closed fist, bloodied.

Your fingers confide in the palm of my hand,
A faith in me.

Epiphany III

Love brought by duskflies bruises the window. (Close the lights, or there'll be no peace!)

And duskflies? Still, a mere notion, love's unattainable. Tonight, in Lielupe's sounding depths fish sleep. On the far coast waves curl back on themselves.

We are poles apart, like birch boughs, pitched north and south. What kind of wind is needed to link us?

We're like barn doors eyeing each other. And a breeze sidles through the barn.

Unattainable love lies under your house. To attain it, the whole house must be torn down. Will you let your house be wrecked, or will you haul it down yourself?

It seemed so simple: duskflies bringing love bruise the window. It seemed simple, blunt, intimate. As if we were birds choraling in the tree-top.

But love lies in the coral, where sounding fish sleep.

In anticipation, the petal flutters.

Though All Our Songs Are Sung

> *Though all our songs are sung,*
> *the bull is still unsung;*
> *sing, girls, the bull song*
> *so cows will run with milk.*
> FOLK SONG

gentle beast
with giant flared nostrils
where's the beautiful beast running? what's wrong with him

what did the gatepost say
post said something to the knife
and then the knife to the arrow in flight

reluctant touch of the gentle beast
to whom did stone speak? stone spoke to glass
and glass weeping with joy, showers

Never So Enraptured

Never so enraptured by a single raspberry,
waking with the morning birds.

Lane of cherries and apples, a peony bed,
twilit fog, and blue heatherfields.
Amen, Annele! You come unto me as a door.
Open as a golden door.

I Seem To Tease Annele

I seem to tease Annele!

– My bounty is
earth-bound, – Annele says.

– But outside the birdhouse in your pine
a thrush sings of Egypt…
And whose song set
steel rails humming?

– Somehow, you're sick.
I'll bear sound children, – Annele says.

– But your frightening dreams?
And hope hidden in the blush on your cheeks?
And who knows why the cuckoo lays her eggs in an alien nest?
And no one sheds the fear of death?
And the bee, dead, in the honey separator?
And the hobo that no particular place on the road heals?
- -
You only ripen and ripen?

Without Whirlwinds

Without whirlwinds this land will be lifeless.
Becalmed, this country will die.
Shrunken fruit falls in the wind,
Strands of flypaper dangle in the air.

Flies stick, and mosquitoes. We twist in the wind.
A cloud of swirling dust and pure pollen.
The flower watches bug-eyed with fear:
Wind whips us past the flypaper once more.

You've missed the point again, Annele says.

A Honed Simplicity

– No, Annele!
A honed simplicity,
thirty-eight branches
three million bristling needles
ride the wind.

Don't only dibble the land.
The space
above the roots must be filled to the sky.
Blessings on you, old taproot, eat the earth, eat!
Can the topmost twig sit idle in the air?
The twig
etches
the enclosing arc!

The Air Is Palpable

The air is palpable,
not empty, but dense.
Birches swapping places at an incredible pace
are palpable,
imperceptible to the eye.
The deafening drone of oaks
bears witness to it all
and when the linden
scoots by me
she leaves
airless space
and bees burned to a crisp.

Button up, Annele, your hooks and eyes, –
we're here for a spell
until torn from our clothes.
Watch wind tear the soul out of the clouds
and launch it at the earth,
splinters of fire!
Button up, Annele, so we don't lose our
lightning.

Clouds

Tonight, – I tell Annele,
let's catch clouds.
But, you've got to set good snares.
Come home
early tonight!

There's no place to put them, – Annele laughs.

What a laugh,
there's got to be a place to put clouds.

I Went Into The Field

I went into the field
and wangled a deal with
my thumb, taking a new tack –
   exulting,
   a skylark gravid in grey:
   look, the whole world grows grey
   before it becomes green.

The Green Fairy Tale

One night, the forest spilled into the city. At first, people didn't know what was going on – on Pērnavas, Ļeņina, Lubānas Street, gas fumes fled down all the streets into the centre of Rīga – breathless and shouting for help. "We're choking!" the fumes cried. "We can't breathe any more!" They said a green mist was seeping into the city from all sides, smelling of pine needles, flowers, of real forest – and it left the city smells queasy, smothering them...

"Save us!" the gas fumes cried, stinking, and sped on.

At midnight, trolley cars rumbling back to sleep in their depot reported the Daugavmala bus station had been taken and all buses were stalled: green moss had crept into their tail pipes, and buses, starting up, sputtered, spluttered, and went dead. The forest wasn't after the trolley buses, only stopping vehicles that polluted the air, harming human air. Right now, it was picking up taxis and other gas guzzlers. And cross-examining dump trucks: what they'd dumped – tin cans, trash, rags – in the forest? The interrogators were juniper bushes, prickly little fellows. They remembered everything – people who yanked out berry bushes, the stalks and all; people who gouged hearts and names into tree trunks; or stripped birch bark off the trees; tore the bark from other trees, or broke bottles. The junipers forgot nothing. Particularly the licence-plates of cars spinning their wheels in the forest, mangling roots, fouling the air.

Swarms of swollen smells in the town centre. Fled from all ends of the city, there was nowhere else to hide. The forest was advancing on all fronts into the city. Only now could people understand how many smells had permeated the city: smells of gasoline and coal smoke, the rest of the smoke smells, all factory smells, garbage smells, cat smells, mold smells, glue smells, liquor smells. Smells hung in the air – scrambling over each other, blathering, blustering, shoving each other – and you could hang an axe in the air it was so thick. Yes, hefting an axe, you could hang it on nothing, the axe suspended in mid-air. The air was already thick as water, so it was hard to walk. You know how hard it is, wading through water when it's up to your belly or breastbone, let alone over your head! The air was thick as water, and over your head. A few boys with inflatable dinghies tried going through the streets in their boats, and succeeded here and there. In the park, frogs leapt into the air but never came back down – staying airborne, leaping from smell to smell. Some people tried jumping from second-floor windows, and nothing happened to them – they landed as if it were water or a mattress, the air a real feather-bed, a mattress of smells – so thick and dense.

Noises, too, fled from the forest to the centre of town. The roar of cars, rattle of trams, pounding of steel hammers, all kinds of clatter and hissing. Clatter is clatter, it never stands still without clattering, it was after a place to clatter. So it plunked down between two utility poles and clattered, so hard everyone's ears shut down. Hissing wheezed through every pipe it could find, like drainpipes down the corners of houses. In a word, noises had been given the heave-ho, and now, fled from their jobs, they didn't know what to do. Banging stomped all over the tin roofs, but clanging hauled a tin tub brimming with empty bottles down the street. Unbearable.

And the dust! The city's dust, afraid of the forest, fled into the centre of town. Penetrated everything. The next morning, the radio's voice was so clogged with dust it hacked and hacked before it spoke. People couldn't hear each other, their ears were clotted with dust, they couldn't wash them anymore, and instead had to use vacuum cleaners. Houses were so evenly blanketed with dust they all looked alike, colorless; the house numbers, layered in dust, were unreadable. People, too, were so evenly covered in dust they all seemed the same, so everyone was amazed that they'd never noticed there was so much dust in the city. A smudge or two on your shoes, in your trouser cuffs, yes – but not such clouds as these!

But the forest pushed closer and closer. A green mist flooded before it. Scent of piné needles and a recent thunderstorm. It slipped into houses through open windows, keyholes, chimneys and air vents, and people began to breathe more easily. It aired the scent of moss and mushrooms, though people still slept unaware of what was happening. But those struggling with insomnia slept sounder than ever before.

The first up was the concierge – to sweep the street – and wonderstruck, she didn't know what to do: the broomstick was sprouting small branches! And the broom itself had leaves! The front door paint had peeled off, the door was thick with evergreen needles.

On the inner doors, too – wherever there were delving wisps of green mist – tiny evergreen needles, buds and branches sprouted and squirmed. The armoire looked like an outsized jungle bush, the chair legs were sending little roots into the floor. Some furniture was overgrown with birch leaves, some with ash, and new shoots were pushing through the floor. In the knitting basket, green vines entwined all the yarn, and the television set was so bushy the concierge took a pair of shears and snipped out a square for the screen, since tonight there was another episode of "At Mrs. Toadstool's". But when she looked out her window, she was dumbstruck: pine trees were shuffling down the street!

Tall, with light brown trunks. And moss slid along the pavement like a green blanket and bilberry bushes, and – what was that? A mushroom? A mushroom! My dears! A fat brown mushroom! The concierge snatched a knife and basket and took off after the mushroom. She caught it in the next block. But then it dawned on her – why run? – mushrooms were coming and coming down the street all by themselves, and she sat on the curb, put her basket beside her, and – the moment a mushroom appeared, she grabbed it and popped it in her basket. What bliss! Soon, the whole street was lined with mushroom pickers, but the forest kept flooding and flowing past like a green river, and the mushroom pickers on the curb looked like fishermen on a riverbank.

Hazelnut bushes came down other streets, their branches elbowing the windows, someone too lazy to go out could pick hazelnuts out his window.

Matchsticks leapt from their matchboxes, mounted each other, inched upward until they were little aspens, since matchsticks are made of aspen wood. Pencils and penholders also assembled and turned into green alders. Skis, sleds, and hockey sticks all greened and budded, but Jānis Lūsis' javelin grew laurel leaves. A war veteran's peg-leg became a little spruce. In the morning, school desks were such thickets that students crawled to their seats. Taller students still had their heads above the bushes, but shorter students disappeared, and when the teacher called on little Jānis, it turned out he'd gotten lost in the branches around his desk and didn't answer – he probably hadn't done his homework. When the teacher called a second time and he still didn't answer, the class searched and found him amoung the leaves under his desk – Jānis had, as the saying goes, "lit out for the woods." The green forest kept coming, coming along the streets, shedding pine needles and leaves in people's hair, beards, handbags and it finally reached the downtown. The fragrant green mist sped from all corners to the centre, and then the great final battle began. The city smells wouldn't surrender. They snapped at the tender tops of pine trees, bit into flowers, withering them. Noises shot through the lingonberries, kicking and trampling, pulling spruces by the ear, whacking mushrooms on the head. Smothering dust swept across the flowers.

But the forest kept coming, coming, with so many blossoms and leaves that noises soon were overgrown with moss. Soft and velvety at first, they still scampered about, but then they got heavier and heavier, until they fell down, green and silent as knolls in the forest. Then, the forest snorted grey city dust through its green nostrils – sneezed, coughed, and the dust was gone, the air was clean and clear green. Only smells still fought on. A swarm of them, many poisonous. Inhaling was the only way the forest could destroy them. But as soon as the pines filled their lungs with gasoline fumes, their treetops wilted. When the birch got a whiff of coal smoke, its bark turned black and everyone could see the birch had breathed its last. Still the forest's green trees fought on, courageously, selflessly.

Wild orchids kept gulping gasoline fumes, dying by the hundreds. Wild cherry trees withered, birches wilted, poisoned rowanberries and acorns fell to the ground, but the forest has got an enormous green life, forest is unconquerable, and toward evening, a juniper bush chomped the last skunky smell in the city. The forest had won.

Then, suddenly as it had come, next night the forest was gone, leaving behind, in the city streets, gateways, and courtyards, green breath. It lived there a long time, until noises and smells reconquered it, but now people know the forest comes to the city at least once a year – a green, green forest...greener than anything else in the world, purer than anything else in the world. Sometimes, when green rain has fallen on the city and green dust floats in puddles on the street, people know it's the pine pollen, and lost in thought they peer into puddles for a long time remembering: the green forest is on its way. Green breath, green eyebrows, green pockets full of green grasshoppers. Green hands cast pocketfuls of green grasshoppers around the post office, the station, stores, the streets. Grasshoppers are hopping and chirring all over the city, and people walk gingerly, avoiding them. Even the trolley stops, the conductor gets out and sweeps a grasshopper off the tracks so it won't get run over. Every year the green forest comes to the city and kills off the stench and reek of the city, silences the noises, destroys dust.

Remember the way the forest spilled into the city last year? When it left, I felt so sad – I wanted to go with it. It'll come again this year. But no one knows when. I was in the forest yesterday. I listened, looked – not a sign. I asked, "Won't you come to the city? Won't you?" Silence. No answer. A big, green forest.

And While A Wee Brown Calf

And while a wee brown calf
trundles through a brown cow,
you too have time
to till the future now.

Hopeless, then fill a vase
full of flower stalks
or fill this evening
with unsaid words.

Or fill this homestead,
this croft and this household
this clan and this land
with filaments of fulfillment.

As the artist sprinkles ink
and the evening amber stars, –
you too have time
to do what's undone, go far.

Marta, Dear Marta

I drove my calves to Uzbekistan.
They didn't drop dead on the spot.
The Uzbek said: The fat's in the pan
with all the calves you've got!

The Uzbek takes the calf's passport,
riffles it like a book of prayers
and tells his pal: – There's nothing to report,
even their calves carry papers.
And are bountifully bucolic
since they don't come down with the colic.
Curious the roads our clans run –
they beget – calves. We beget – children.

You better believe it. Our wives
care for calves, hens on their perch,
plough, drain, sow and scythe
so the GNP's safe as a church.

So I thought: make no mistake,
our women are always tendered
to something, our determined donation rendered
to the communal affairs of the state.

That made me think, maybe
we're all out of whack,
for any child in tack
takes up the nation's slack.

So I dropped by Marta's door.
– Marta, dear Marta, I implored.
There's a question stuck in my craw,
stranger than any country saw.

44 *

See, after I herded the cattle
I said: Beast, in what kind of fettle
does a body feel as she rousts
a huge herd around the house?

Marta, wise to my ways,
and my comic turns of phrase,
sidles up to me and says:
– So, be quick, we can't dawdle all day! –

I give her the low-down on what's up.
Say: Tup and tickle, tickle and tup.
– But I can't abandon the calves,
no one's duty's done by halves.

Cocking a crooked grin, Marta says – Fat chance.
Men are all cheek and talk.
I got no time to cakewalk
around the barns and bairns, and dance.

So what can you do? Dally and dicker? –
Marta's eyes are flaring embers,
– The nation needs another nipper,
so fiddle a poem about a family member. –

Snatch a glance at Marta's shoulder.
So bent and so abused,
so it goes, happenstance enfolds her.
So it goes, as of old, confused.

But Marta sprints away, sprightly and tall.
She's neither unwilling nor uppity.
She's got no time, no time at all.
She carries sweetgrass for the calves, not me.

The Single Sin of Adams

Adams stained by a single sin:
he fell in love with Ieva.
Then, Ieva and Adams fell in
line before God.

God said: "Heavens above,
Adams, why'd you do that? You knew
God is love."
Adams said: "No, I am too!"

"You scamp, purdah's
too good for you!" God bellowed.
"How could you sink so low –
that flat-assed wench, Ieva!"

Adams shot back: "We fell as low
as your own rainbow:
you call that a vice,
and snatch back Paradise?"

The Lord threw them out, pocketed Paradise.
Whoopee! So now, thank God,
we can play around at odds
and ends with our wives.

Flipping fig-leaves into the air,
we undo Ieva's hair:
our only sin in God's eyes,
passed down to us from Paradise.

We'll never see Eden again.
But wait a minute, listen:
Adams' sin is sweet surprise,
our truest taste of Paradise.

Yes, She Was A Madonna

Yes, she was a madonna. I wasn't
the first under the sun to figure this out.
I saw this years later in paintings as she cradled
a child, Mother of God, light banding her head,
and I remember the heat of her breasts
in my hair. Yes, – there she was.
I looked at the Mothergod's hands,
thinking her fingers are as lovely
as the woman's across the way.

Our neighbor moved
but before going
she held me so close
I still feel the heat in
the hollow of her thighs
on my forehead.
A long time later, the ritual repeated
(another story; childhood gone).

As she stepped through the door, grandmother
muttered to no one at all:
– There's a girl that'll come to no good,
they'll strip her clean as butter bowl. –

Why bother about all this now?

Since then, I've seen her several times,
off in the distance, dimly.
Striking eyes, beatific smile,
but a solid, sensible stride.
Wingless. My heart ached.
Somebody else draped in butterflies
swayed, a violin in the night,
but suddenly her soul whinnied like a mare.
I leapt back, stood still.

How women long: loss
in every star. Under a street lamp
a girl slimmed and snaked her hips,
another boosted her breasts
but still, she has no cleavage.
O makeup, mask the mundane.

I come across her petals everywhere,
but have no time or strength
to gather them. Still, I know,
I know she's out there.

Epiphany IV

We brushed by each other. Circle by circle. Sphere by sphere. Locus unknown. Not yours, not mine. Wheel cycling on asphalt. Asphalt cycles under the cycling. Wind skimmed water, skimmed the wadi, unaware of secret springwells. Soothing hand on the brow, fondled breasts, a hip held, no stroking of the spirit.

Tree didn't root into tree, nor stone into stone.

We flitter along the surface, touching here, there, all of us. But kept good space between us. Gaps in a stone pile.

– That seems to ensure easy action, less friction, less resistance. – Ball-bearings said so.

Yes, we agreed – ease ensures less resistance. Taught by ball-bearings, we forgot ball-bearings weren't born to lose their bearings.

And again – sphere brushes by sphere, circle by circle. Disc by disc, somersault by somersault.

And our motion is a feckless cycling. And our cycling is feckless recycling. And our recycling is a feckless circling.

But in the field, a child plucks dandelions and loops the stems, linking one with the other, his first homemade chain hung around her neck. Spurred on, in the blood.

By The Roadside

I pause by the roadside. There were houses here once.
I scribble a song
of cold ovens and
cinders with a chunk
of old coal on chimney steles, a song
of cats without their corner
and children with mother's corpse.
Scribble a song with coal
snatched from this rubble.

Folks, don't haul down
the last chimney steles,
let squandered lots lie where
untended apple trees take root in the rubble!
Let hops creep through grass
looking for their staves,
the yard and footpaths overgrown
with rose and lilac shoots!

Scribble of luck poured
into the tureen on New Year's Eve,
of sprucewood sparks
in the wide bread oven,
the loaf's smell
and the little baked rolls
of leftover dough.

There were households here.
Ashes turn to blossoms,
bricks take root in the grass, pain
in plots of remembrance.
I won't be here tomorrow
but this afternoon, wounded, I scribble
over the chimney steles
with old coal.

Enfold me, ink fish

I

Enfold me, ink fish,
in the blue evening!
Aie, your blue vales,
aie, the hazy blue vales!

A pale moon flower –
aie, in the blue evening!
Nipped in the sea's navel
in the blue evening.

As molten mountains belch smoke,
as fog sleeps in the topmost twigs –
ink fish, blot
my word this evening!

II

And ink fish blotted my word
and thus spake increased words.

III

And ink fish blotted my word
from familiar shores,
and peeled stamps from letters,
and the letters wended their own way.

And ink fish blotted my word,
and I bored inward.
Boring as if you knew the springwell's source,
as if you knew the stone itself
       sparked by the clanging horseshoe,
the very moss into which someone will cast the fire seed,
some nerd or Nero
or nervous Nelly.

And ink fish blotted my word
from familiar shores,
and I forsook palms and psalms,
the sartorial and serpents, and outside
all such, or more acutely, inside –
yes, inside, I trailed
cloud, fog, into the
whirlwind pulling inward.

Pilgrim Stone

We'll root this cellar out of the earth,
hoist it overhead, a skycage for birds,
or turn a skein of sky-blue smoke
into umber peat,
or a cranberry. Who could quarrel with that?

No stone is static, or perpetual.
I saw stone climb a tower,
it braided a nest among black crows,
and hatched dappled stones, fledglings.
Who later learned to fly.
Why should pilgrim stones
in the sky dazzle your eye?

O, spring is myrtle green,
and back from warmer climes,
pilgrim stone sings in the birch by the cage.
Sings its flight, charmed,
        sings flight.

To Meet A Stone

I

skirt a ravine
meet a stone
the sideling stone
a crony

on either side
set stones
and stay inside

then show a single
stone the soil
transplant
plant

weed and hoe
weed and water
the single stone

till it moans
till it glisters
and
a flower erupts
in the core

hardening blossoms
begin to
peel

as bees
sheath the blossom
with more water

as fruit evolves
oscillating the head
bracing

as the fruit's
freshening air grows
ticklish
seeds
grow
dusty

touch the heart
task the heart

and survive
by taking stone's
heavy seeds
to heart

II

Coils compressed in stone – my sleepless stone.
Unsprung coils in stone – my sleepless stone.

    Not riverbottom of redfins, nor
    seaweed, nor the apple core's worm – no one sleeps.

Stone gathering – day in, day out.
Stones sprout inward – day in, day out.

    Outbound bird, smoke
    outbound, but not you.

No other escape, escape is inscape.
No other wit, only inwit.

    Winsome as a wagtail flying
    inward – so stone flies.

III

Let's not discuss stone.
Not a word. Stone is holy.
I see a grey stone rise over the hill,
as others see the sun rise.

– A gray stone? And up there,
as the clock strikes twelve?
– Yes, stone mounts our sky,
as others track the circling sun.

– And grey?
– Yes, absolutely grey.
– Well then, you've got only a gleam of light.

– No, sages taught me
how its light disperses.

– Where are sages teaching that?
– Track them down in the fog
and ask rain-driven rye!
Question the dark stubble field.

(In the field a tortured quail
crawls into mother's cast-off cloak.)
– But back to the stone – where does it go?
And after all how does it begin to shed light?
– Such a color – it's indescribable.
You'd have to speak more Latvian.

IV

O, stone speech
isn't mangled at all
sound asleep under water
it will rise

stand for hours
listening by the riverside
for one single
stone word

Among One's Own

among one's own
you, stone and you, stone

we carp
we share silence

in thankfulness I am
silent   among
you.

Bilberries Blueing

Bilberries blueing: I remember:
one day Annele said:
gypsies were on the road: picking bilberries.
Aren't you writing poems any more?

But the jays are here,
and one day Annele says:
the jays are everywhere,
they cluster in the hazel trees, caper and caterwaul.
Aren't you writing poems any more?

And old lady Apars says: gathering storks are flocking
in the ploughed fields.
Apparently they've pecked one stork to death:
storks in summary session.

Annele again: – Aren't you writing poems any more?

And Night Attends Me

By day I sleep
and dream of sweating gleaners,
feeling neither shiftless
nor guilty.
By night I weed my words,
selecting from my seedlings
in the crowded soil's cryptic text
my several roots.

Gorging herself all day,
the cow ruminates all night.
Each dark hour's density
a stomach
tumbling to what the tongue
has torn up, lush, insatiable, tasteless,
tuft after tuft.
The meadow's asleep, gleaners sleep.
And night attends me.

Epiphany v

Nothing's easier than travelling blind by dark. In the daylight, driven by doubt, you keep to the wheel ruts of others, their spoor and markings, their footprints, or ponder for a long time: should I chance it? – go, or forgo?

Were earlier passersby any wiser? It's beyond you, clinging safely to the beaten track. But after a couple of kilometres it doubles back – so you see, everybody took this road on trust, and all came back deceived. A looping rut to nowhere.

Daylight, the cross-purposes of crossroads, doubtful directions, a spilt drop unravelling. I slip into night, nothing simpler than travelling blind, trusting my feet, eyes – I've nothing else at night in the dark. Daylight? The beaten track, tried by others, and true. Roads are other people's experience, trails others took. But at night, only my own experience, my own route.

Above all, I avoid lights and lighted windows. If you're out at night, don't look at a well-lit window! You'll come away dazzled, unable to see. Like a dog who's lost his sense of smell. I determinedly detour around lights.

Darkness is dense and beautiful, and trusting myself I trust darkness, as it entrusts itself to me. If you've swum in ocean swells, you'll know. Darkness is like the sea: drift into the deep, absorb the sea's grandeur, the grandeur of darkness, and you're confident.

Cleaving darkness, I wonder if I glow, not seeing it, unaware, and surely someone somewhere thinks I'm a tiny firefly. Not God: – I'm a materialist, but maybe Destiny. Then I wonder: slashing through the underbrush, the daily route close by: Can he see me? Is Destiny smirking? Does he see me stumble into the ditch? Or skirt its edge? Did he dig the ditch?

Then, flooded with strength, I laugh at him. A mere dot in the darkness – I sharpen my sense of smell, peel my eyes, and stride past the ditch. I cannot stumble, because seeking affirmation of the self in the dark is an affirmation unlike any other.

Darkness, my vitamin. I breathe darkness like oxygen and darkness burns in me.

Walking at night, I feel the way darkness loves me. A pine tree singles me out to the right; scent of resin in the darkness to the left, and overhead, the faint rustle of pine cones where stars should be between a bough's fingers, but there are – thank goodness! – none. A branch slashed my cheek, confirmed my existence, and when I stubbed my toe on a root it recognized and, in its own way, saluted me.

Tempted to test yourself, go into darkness, alone. While all may be lost in the dark – you'll find yourself.

You've got your feet with you, wise and understanding – familiar with stones and moss and mud and brittle twigs. You've got your hands with you: reach to the right – juniper, to the left – oak, as you seek affirmation.

You've got your eyes and ears with you. Aspen quivers, but even in snow, the oak refuses to shed its leaves.

Your darkness surrounds you – immense, infinite. What more do you need?

My Love Was So Mute

My love was so mute,
my touch so insensible
its star died that year,
inostensible.

The stone is still here. Discreet, unseen,
turned mossy, green and olden;
no matter how keen
you won't discern the gem.

Epiphany VI

Each day has a given name. It bobs up as a melodic motif, surfaces, seizes control and haunts me.

Wood chips...

A truck went down the street, the wind sucked shavings from the load of lumber and swept dust by me on the breeze.

A shaving disappeared down a sliver of endless city space, but since then the day's been filled with fragrance. To me, sawdust is the quintessence of life. It's no surprise that I link the smell of green shavings to a particular coffin that stood in the granary loft stuffed with shavings, and we knocked out the knotholes. We played sailor boys in the loft, and grandfather's death didn't seem so sad: he shipped out, went down to who knows where – in his final cradle, scent of sawdust and shavings lingering in the air.

I love the spiral swirl of shavings. They conjure up dervish dancers, the bolero, cha-cha.

Shavings curlicue like tendrils of hops, conceit twirls on the tips of moustaches; and corkscrew piglet tails tend to cheer me up.

That's why I can work so hard. Because shavings reek of work. I remember the old master boatbuilder in our village. His cap, his room and even his dog reeked of shavings.

Out on the walk, I'd watch his bit bore into a log, turning out swirls of wood, and old Miklāvs would say, – Now, my boy, I'll set you a riddle: what d'you call a toddling ram that shits in toddling circles?

The smell of wood chips and smoked pilchard always blend in my mind. Huge mounds of wood chips in the factory fish yard, and we three boys, perched on a mound, snapping down cards, with the sea beyond the fence, screeching gulls in the blue, but below where they do the weighing, salting and smoking, billows of smoke, and the watchman cursing like a trooper says he'll tan our hides. Mother smelled of wood chips and smoked pilchard, and so did grandmother; I suspect all great-grandmothers in the everlasting stroll around cowled in the smell of wood, smoke pilchard for old Peter.

Chipboard is all the current rage. What a violation, vicious. Imagine the chips of a tree lying down beside chips from another tree in a presswood sheet, alien pulp, cemented by synthetic glue in some press, this glue the only bond that binds, nothing else. Like a couple at cross-purposes, or friends who've calculated their affairs.

It's crystal clear, this glue's got a different formula. And moreover, this formula for inorganic matter is much simpler than mine. But sawdust is an organic compound. The formula for oaken sawdust hasn't been figured out, not yet. The birch shaving is my sister, both of us alive and organic. In tapping season, I recognize and respect this shaving as it is bored from the birch's living flesh. Let the shaving rot by the roots of its tree, moulder and melt into sap and rise up through the branches once more. As for panelling, who could love such pulp. A mechanical composite. Flat. And most disgusting – the glue – that seals it together, synthetic and inorganic. I like a wood strip that retains its inherent quality when torn from its tree. A woven basket has no glue, no nails...taper plaited to taper, all of the same tree. And that's beautiful!

I respect the tapers crackling and burning to ash as much as the pine tree itself.

As I loll about on a mound of wood chips, each chip breathes – breathes freely, confidently. It's just like delegates from trees in the general assembly of an alien world.

I suspect they'll each defend their own trees in sorting yards, sawmills and the lumber mills of the United Tree Organization.

No one will be allowed to heave a larch into the river, drowning raftwood; the larch is our land's heaviest tree, the river will suck it down.

Ash won't be sold for firewood, not while so many pine spade and axe handles wobble and split. Sliver of chestnut defends the chestnut's right to mosaic leafing, little and large leaves interlocked, though birch and fir can't comprehend that sort of thing. Meanwhile, tendrils of weeping birch are free to droop, which is why, if we listen to its slivers, this is the world's most beautiful birch tree.

Lolling on a mound of wood chips, I seem to be in a forest, thousands of trees around me, and so, if I were a sliver, just a naked little sliver, I'd still keep my character, since I'm the sliver of a great rooted tree.

A crow caws on a dead branch, but a sap-bottle hangs from a supple bough. I watch men carrying saws, augers and axes. They're going into the woods. Chips are flying. The world is full of sawn wood and sawdust. To me wood chips are the vital signs of life.

Mother

But mother's the heart of this poem about milk.
You, too, shall see this come to pass.

A circle binds this world – eternal:
wherever you're bound you'll find – mother.

Follow the bumble bee, butterfly,
even your own oriole, it all
returns to mother. Go wherever you want,
covet the coveted, seek what is sought, attain
and not attain, but what
you failed to find is sought
in mother, and everything attained returns
to mother, or becomes mother.
Mother is, all in all.

Perhaps this must be felt, not fathomed:
in the ease of pacifying, peaceable flesh.
I don't remember her smooth breasts –
neither the heft nor heat,
but in streets, carnivals – and sanctuaries:
I look life dead in the eye –
women breathing, the serpentine
swirl of their designs,
dances, pillows and dandelions.

Perhaps this must be felt, not fathomed,
as women leave the sauna on holy eve:

First, mother shaped like an empty old
jeroboam in miraculous evening
bloom, as if someone
will once more knead dough at dawn.

Then the middle sister – a peony
with summer solstice in the stamen,
will leave the window ajar again
and stare and not weep into the dark.

And on her heel – an elder sister, engaged
but unable to endure men more fragile than she,
so parries and prevaricates.
Married, she'll show no mercy.

And as for Ildze's eyes, they're meadow birds,
and her voice – she'll love you so well
you'll think your sackcloth is silk.

It's Good You Lie Afar

It's good you lie afar,
they say: it heals annealing.
But I see your pale face
in the blue.

>   (It's very far.
>   Defies thought.)

It's good, you lie afar,
beyond fretfulness.
But someone soaks his head
in the black river of your hair.

>   (So unbearably near.
>   So unbearable,
>   I don't know where to hide my eyes.)

I Read Smoke Carefully

I read smoke carefully
smoke's of two minds
shreds of shroud
or threads of swaddling

I read smoke carefully
almost impossible to translate
there are no smoke
words in our tongue

On Lush Summer Sundays

On lush summer Sundays
churchyards lie in the morning hills
watered and fresh
as our garden plot.

Seeded a moment ago, and planted
with armfuls of flowers,
and –
    may father rest in peace! –
hoe and weed, weed and hoe
(Help along the cemetery hybrid.)

Lush summer Sundays,
lush and tenacious life,
lush and tenacious, we lead our
children to the churchyard.

The watering can still shines,
prime.

Epiphany VII

We can't crowd death. We never nudge aging. We seek ourselves. Our Separate Self.

Life is two people approaching each other. My age musters my youth. They meet in maturity. On the rim of maturity.

Like two billy goats locking horns on a log spanning a river, I'll meet myself. A blessed butting! Horned, they're bound to hunker towards each other, on the plank.

I'm meeting up with myself all the time. When my grey beard meets my nursery nipple, I'll be most myself. When mountain snow meets Nile crocodiles.

Like two parliamentarians, North Pole approaches South Pole. I'll locate me on the equator.

As palm presses palm, I'm me at the moment of applause. I am two trembling palms in space. Such is the solemnity, perhaps, in applause.

Blending new cream with old butter in a mixing bowl, there's a moment when butter and cream are neither, the moment buttermilk separates, new butter begins.

We don't age, we verge on new cream.

Be ye old as the full moon, you can be whipped into the new, if you know you must be whipped by the light of the crescent moon.

Tears are only whey.

Earth Mother

Beet leaves
big brainy ears
absorbed the sun's
word: eat and be fat, fecund;
munificent Earth Mother, lay
a hand on my brow, on all the living.

I Could Stay Out Here For Years

I look in on a collective farmer
and tell the milkers: good day!
Are you always on the udder,
making milk instead of hay?

Better skip the quips,
or some handyman'll nick
me with his tongue: – Hey, loose lip,
you sporting a stickpin or tallystick?

What bunk. What tripe.
But will they bunk me down for the night?
Country silence rings in my ears.
I could stay out here for years.

– Where? Here? This agro-farm?
    – Sure, right here ...
– Why?
    – Why not? If it's OK with you ...
I like calves with floppy ears
and cows – when they moo.

– Moo?
    – Sure, and the way they cud,
so content, I feel like cudding, too.
– But work'd better be in your blood,
or the brass'll get beaten out of you.

– Sure, sure, I'll do my bit.
But not all the time.
Whatever the work, it should be split –
you do yours and I'll do mine.

Since everyone's got his domain,
I'm a poet.
    – Sweet Jesus' name,
Alda... We're in the silk!
Nurse him nice with warm milk!
And you better not smoke in bed...

    – I don't
– 'cause our sheaves are stacked in the shed.
But maybe you're gonna write about us?
– O papa, he's uproarious!
– So, what brings you here?
You on the run from home?
– Look, girls, he's got no gear,
travelling clean as a bone.

(Uproarious, stickpin ... Don't be surprised by citified words on the farm. Felicita Ertnere, when visiting the countryside in the 1920s, recalled how she had ventured into the yard at dawn, where a girl was polishing milk cans. The young actress wants to engage in conversation, and says: – I wonder should today be sunny? The sun and clouds are betwixt and between.
– Yes, like Leonardo da Vinci lighting, – says the girl.)

And they led me off to the hay ricks.
And laughing Alda says: – my good man
You'll bed down here with us hicks
Like them holy shepherds in Bethlehem.

- -

The likes of them lack a trousseau,
They're stuck with grandmother's dower,
an embroidered meadow to mow,
a motley blanket of madder.

I took a snooze in God's nostril,
old hay, but still with a tang
that's tart and shrill,
though God don't sniff worth a dang.

Me neither.
Asleep.

Handlebars

Man, I got hopped up handlebars in my hand
with miles and miles to go –
a lonesome long ride, man,
a bust-out,
a break from what I got
to where I got to get.
What with a wall called cosy living
cutting us off from the world I want.
Where a minute comes on like an hour.
And no putting in time fixing the times.
And a moment whacks you in the face
   like a hailstone
   like in love
   like in pain.
And highways and byways and backwater silence,
easy bends in sleepy roads.
No, man – you got to handle the handlebar,
loop and dip between the trees.
Hill. Down in the gully, sheen of shifting sands.
Speed. A lot of men'll go down here...
Hold on to holding on!

Nothing yanks those bars out of my hands!
The bar's got a beat all its own – gear down.
The bar's got a beat all its own – gear round!
Man, roads that slide by so easy
let's give them the slip.
This cross-country haul
will wire you up and wear you down.
Man, we got no time to chew the fat,
This old bus is byway-bound ...
Man, you do what you got to do?

And Though I've Been Brazen

And, though I've been brazen on the road,
I shied away from her house, from
asking for water, a drink.
So, maybe I'll suggest
cultivating air gardens
of sugarbeet clouds, Zeppelin pumpkins!
I could promise to
build a tower in the yard – with triple doors,
portals at all compass points;
facing hops, hunting and honey fields,
facing meadows quick with quail and quicksand,
facing fields along the Euphrates and Tiber...

I'd breed bats and owls for her
full of the knowledge of darkness...

Four days slipped away, and I
still couldn't get up the gumption to go
through the gate.
But by the evening of the fifth day,
the earth around me moaned a little.
I went in. The setting sun fell into my eyes.

    They homesteaded here together:
    old Ķurvis was weaving a basket by the kindling box.
    – Good evening! – Good evening! Annele's at home...
    A motorcycle stood by the house.
    I sat side-saddle,
    propped against the weathered
    log wall.
    And the sun set.
    The sauna stood down by the pond.
    I might live there.

Hay has to be brought into the mudroom,
no, straw would be better,
and by the small window
an old table,
for writing.

She didn't come out.
I knocked, but she didn't appear.
Ķurvis said: – Go on in –
I went and rapped
on the inner door,
but no one appeared.

I sat in the old chair at the old table
and left her a letter.

Ķurvis sidled up and said: – She's sleeping.
She sleeps on soothing nights like this.
Today's Milda's Day.
tomorrow's Valija's,
but Klāvs' was yesterday –

Ķurvis had a screw loose, learning the old calendar by heart.

Butterflies

Butterflies
are airborne sky flowers
unable, Ildze said,
to settle down, shed
their petals.

No, Inese says, the butterfly's
a tease.
As he flits about,
we all turn featherbrained.

Another Idiot Evening

Another
idiot evening –
hats slumped on their pegs,
and the heart inquires
after rhinoceroses on their last legs.

*

And beside the barn,
shelled oats and barley –
O! – under the linden tree
I see a keening monkey.

*

No such foul fate
lies on the shelf –
a pale closet hangs
itself from the wall.

*

Standing on her fallen arches,
the pregnant star mourns
but only a cucumber is born
a mottled bottle-green.

– So, you're ready to take off, Annele says.
You always take more chances than me.

– Sure, my friends corral dinosaurs!

Epiphany VIII

Sometimes I suspect God is working out with me as if I were a soccer ball. Hauls back his leg and hoofs me in the ribs. (How does God get his kicks after all!) Who knows where the goal is, how do I know who he plays with? He could've suited me up with the devil or Firsov or Pelé, or with the boys over there in the yard, but him – no, he's off playing one-on-one with himself. Archangel Michael's the goalie, but God doesn't kick me into the goal, since I might keep on rolling, out into the world. God never stoops to play with mortals. So he body-checks me a bit, elbows me aside, and dumps me down in the flowers of paradise until next time. It's as boring as sin! Abounding flowers, pomegranates, the anemone blues. But the stadium rattles my dreams, roaring, the goalie's leg broken. Even flowers aren't manured here, fertilized by God's grace; there's not even a piddling puddle for the soccer ball to plop into, wallowing like a pig. It's so tempting to hope God will haul back once and boot me up under the sheltering white wing of an angel – sugar candy in tissue paper.

He's barefoot, of course, but God can't break his toes; still, I wish he had real cleats, real soccer boots and someone else to play with! But God plays alone, determinedly, decidedly alone. God's soccer is a lonely lonely game. Lonely for us both: lonely for God, even lonelier for God's soccer ball. No outs, no penalty shots, no fighting close to the goal. Nothing.

They don't know the damnedest thing about rugby in heaven.

Epiphany IX

You can't get what you want when you want it in this world. A recklessly arranged world. A non-arranged world. – Wait, they say. – Wait, wait.

It's long hard haul. Wait for the trolley. Wait for boiling spuds. Wait to get to heaven. But they won't let me. They say: – Wait! You've got to live out your life.

The world is weaned on waiting, endless entreaties, wait, wait. Mother waits for her child, a lass waits for love, the meritorious citizen waits for a medal, the martyr waits for deliverance. Wait, be patient. And while you're suffering patiently, time stands still and instils waiting. Each moment in time grows indolent, a lazybones lying in wait. He waits for the next moment – but strange, we step back. To get closer, you must step forward – don't wait until it comes to you. They say: – Wait, morning's wiser than evening. A lazybones shelters in the saying: – Never do today what you can put off till tomorrow. Thus, tomorrow moves back by one day. Is the future a giant crab scuttling backwards, crawling toward us?

Shall we embrace the future, going after it, or will the future fall back on us? Wait, the future will arrive on your doorstep. Wait, the goal's chasing the football, the target will appear begging for the bullet. Wait! Patiently! Patient. Restrained. Hang in, your time will come.

Sure, just like your coffin's coming. It's sure to come. To carry you off, traipsing backwards.

"All good things come to him who waits," says the proverb. Haw!

The Poem Began

The poem began with
mother's milk in my mouth.
I felt no guilt, so I was beaten.

They murdered the mother elk,
her teats still leaking milk.
I couldn't eat her meat,
and they beat me.

The faithful relish
holy communion,
affirm their lives
in, with, and under
Christ's blood.

Blood
validates the vendetta.

I speak of brothers bonded
by milk, the obligations of milk.

A suckling is born clean
with nothing to brag about:
he's merely a milksop.

In his marrow, the suckling
milks his mother's esteem,
his integrity hers.

– Call down the crone!
Call her an old hag! –
He can't.
He's a milksop to the bone.

Milk

I love milk, like autumnal fog
seeping over the fields.
But my tongue is still moist
with stars – from the Milky Way.

May my star
never deliver slivers.

When I was Still Small

I noticed her a long time ago,
when I was still small – I had an inkling
of something hidden from me.

The woman across the way was a beautiful lake.
As a tot, she often let me toy
with her fingers.

I thought she might be my mother
though mother seldom went in for fondling,
too used to me, I suppose.
The woman across the way dandled me on her knee
and let me play with her fingers.

I clung like a burr,
(childless) she clung to me.
Curled in her lap I felt the heat
of her breasts in my hair.

Soothed by her breathing,
I slowly sank, sank into her.
Suddenly I remembered swaying trees in the marsh
and the bog where we went cranberry picking,
so afraid I caught the folds in her dress.

She flexed, belly firm.
I rose like a breath of air
drifting to sleep in the hull
of a golden sloop, clutching her finger.

Later, I sang a lot – boat songs –
my own tune and tempo:
... A skiff asway on the water,
seeking the ploughman'a daughter...They say:
– What kind of song is that, my sweet? I didn't know
then, or now. It must be mine
but it's likely hers.

Hard On her Heels

Mother, I followed
hard on her heels
into hollows I'd never seen,
deeper than potato drill or grave.
Deep, where children sleep in the dark.

This Is Her Cairn

This is her cairn
a cast-iron kettle
a cast-iron kettle scraped clean
come with spoons,
beat your breast with spoons
say you didn't
want it this way.

Cross your spoons
and bear in mind
you are brothers of one bowl,
brothers of one kettle.
O, pilgrims bearing spoons –
bow down your heads!
And plant
your spoons
around her cairn. –
A graceless flower.
Full of grace.

We all go
to our mother's cairn
carrying white spoons.

At Maruža's Again

A big full faced moon.
The crone comes, casts horse beans into the sty.
      Apparition of a water
      jug in a dream –
      promise of health.

Thunder carting blown-up Huns along the horizon.
The old man gets up, takes the axe and hurls it into the whirlwind.
      The dreamt room
      decorated with flowers –
      promise of burning.

The elder sister is led to bloom, the middle led to bloom, the youngest bursts into blossom, flings her wreath into the spruce.
      Someone strode through snow in
      the dream with wooden legs –
      life among cold people.

On the other side of night, girls unlock the corral, scatter grass for the cows, fernseeds, full of hope.
      And dreamstruck by stars –
      beans will grow.

Throw ribbons, throw flowers into the stream from the bridge!
At the wedding, throw money onto the clean-napkin-covered plate!
        If a moon rises in your dreams
        – a son will be born;
        if a dream cucumber is eaten
        fruitless work.

The blacksmith hammers in the sky, the woodpecker hammers in the pine.
Throw money, throw money into the coffin, so it won't come back!
        You bought milk –
        you'll make friends with children.

Like an ember, Maruža glows like an ember in evening skies.
Such nonsense! Utter nonsense! – But – let there be more!

Absolutely insane! Of course, of course,
        but broomhandles
        twirl inside their skins.

Foolishness? How do I know!
        Who's to ask?
        Witches are burnt.

Latvia, O Butter Churn

Winter winds may blow,
we've mown the meadow
and stuffed our stables with hay
to the gable window.

Our abundant grain
drives other men insane.
Don't look now, the masticating cow
hears milk in her ears.

Latvia, O chock-full and sweet sister,
O butter churn
bursting at the seams,
your chin dripping cream.

Bulging stores, bulging belly, litre and tonne!
Women caring for calves sing the centuries.
Down arduous years
Māra braided the blossoms of her ancient wreath through
the cow's horns.

> God go with you
> in ancestral moors;
> there'll be other drovers
> but no such singers.

– Balderdash, – Marta says.
– We sing in a double quartet!

– O Marta! The city's forgotten our folk songs,
The threat's in Rīga.
Choristers counting notes on choral sheets.
Riga's tuned out on transistors.
Why mimic that chary, witless
chanteuse?
Why brush off the clan's beauty for grass in a greener glen?
Mother dear, you may draw pure milk from the teat
but the song your daughter sings is watered down.

        But the enduring, undiluted word
        sleeps unknown,
        unsoured, –
        thine is abounding power unbound.

where
   fellside cows, fellside bulls;
where
   my brother's bucking cow is shucking flies, there's no
   buck-shucking by the cow across the road: it teeter-totters;
where
   the butter god blessed me; I piled a heap of butter
   buttressed by slabs of cheese;
where
   sleepyeyes let her clan's cows lie down
   in the lee of the woods;
where
   my calves had old hair on their hides;
where
   my wee cows loomed like pert hens
   in weeny eggs!
where...where...where...

Catch A Neutral Apple

catch a neutral apple
if you can

they've all resisted
the sodden earth
and fallen soundly

these green seedlings
show
a neutral apple
can never be

I Love A Floating Apple

I love a floating apple in the night.
Treeless, twigless,
I love the floating apple tree in the night,
rootless, weighing down branches in the night.

And the whole earth, afloat in the night
neither borne nor braced by anyone
I love darkness – that doesn't disappear
as I wake again

But keeps a distance, unseen
and then, as the sun sets, draws near.
I see someone approaching:
emerging from the dark, merging into the dark again.

O, A Candle Burns

O, a candle burns,
O, a candle burns beautifully.
The flame quickens, flickers white.
And dispels darkness. Then – dispels light.
And God crosses the devil for my soul.

But a candle burns,
O, a candle burns beautifully.
Scampering wind shivers my flame.
Paraffin pours over the candle's lip,
someone sits for my dying.

But a candle burns.
O, a candle burns white!
Darkness curls its petal head:
burning white, end to end,
wick drowning in paraffin.

But something glisters wanly.
Something glistens, gleaming wanly.
Candlelight in my eyes.
Ahead, in celestial stalls,
God crosses the devil for candle souls.

Trio

Pauline, past fifty, feels
she's in a season of second growth.
Buds in her pores, ripe for a tumble in the ricks.
And says:
I'd not only give my reaper
a white shirt
I'd lay down my white soul.

Poppy audacious flower,
beneath a full moon
never looks back.
She leaves behind
replete rye
and weeping cornflowers.

Thunder pounds his fists.
All his pounding splutters in space.
Like some shiftless father –
making a monthly
call on his children –
he'll love them to death.

Epiphany x

Breeze of blighted flowers. The strong don't feel it.

Breeze of blighted flowers. Chatterboxing daisies on the phone. Clover gave her such a steamy look. Coltsfoot feels the same about fool's parsley.

Breeze of blighted flowers, falling petal in the night. An apparent fluke, one by one. So imperceptible.

No one will tell you how it happens. So you won't notice, every flower hides the first fallen petal. She'll shift the rest so it seems none are missing. And you won't see the second fallen petal either.

Only meadowrue has swept the night skies with white wreaths. And, sapped by the night, sleeps soundly all day. Earth petals fall and turn white at her feet. Everyone sees it. But she sleeps shamelessly.

Nothing, nothing's seen, not in the blossom, the stem, the leaf, but the breeze of blighted flowers, I tell you, walks the meadow.

And no one believes that's the way it is. The strong don't feel, the weak never confess: – it gives them pain.

Still, the nights are so lovely as meadowsweet dances in the skies. And worn out, sleeps all day.

After all, in a while it's – only hay.

Pea Children

Pea children
revelling in childhood.
Small rows of seven in a ripening pod
hear in the festal garden,
an old seed carrot harping
on the correct collective feel.
But it was no secret to the small pea
that as the pod pops
every one will go
his own which way.
The reaping
moment
ripens.

Epiphany XI

Sometimes I remodel cemeteries. These days, expecially in these parts, they are very beautiful but I end up mulling over the paltriness of life. What do death and birth dates divulge? Asinine arithmetic, subtraction of two four-digit numbers. The sum of human life in double digits: 25, 60 or 83 – whoever – the addle-pated or adept, politician or pickpocket. They say: here lies Kārlis at rest, he put in 52 years, with mourners in his wake. And all the Justīnes, Mudītes, Alfrēdi and Miķeļi lined up behind him rest in peace, put in a few years, too, and are mourned. Avowals of shared sorrow, a bald cemetery sentence. Always the same: "The dear departed live in the memory of the bereaved." O, this abysmal, bland indexing! So, in our concordances of cross and stele, we reveal only an incapacity for remembrance. Or were the deceased doomed to such bland stone formulae. Imagine a cross-reference index with only

1. name, surname
2. lifespan
3. to the memory of, in deep sympathy, mourn...

No sign, word, rubric, or code, though a whole life's been buried, a complete encyclopedia! Mourn at home, dear mother!

I yearned for far fields
Heard the larks' singsong
Darkness fell,
The heart stilled.

He yearned, we all yearn. Mourn at home, mother dear! But let your son's star repose on the grave! Since he had one. Let his gleeful cry repose on the grave! Since he had one. If he didn't, then lay out his anger. This is the public cemetery, I'm here for my dead. I want to know: what tongue of fire touched him? He knew neither boundless joy nor tongues of fire. Perhaps, then, the bookworm, or soccer player's pang?

He felt deeply, she strongly. His beautiful face, her beautiful heart. He was mellifluous, so erect a stone rostrum, or a gaping mouth where well-wishers can lay wreaths and flowers. All his life, he collected friends – and she – beer bottle labels. Wreath his name in friendly names, who, if they're not spooked by stones, won't mind. Cover her grave with labels, the root of her life. Let's go into the cemetery as if it were a huge exposition of sensuality and insight, the motto over the gates: CREDO. The People's Trade Exhibition in Mežaparks can't hold a candle to this huge exposition of All Souls, – it's a drab, one-shot, once-in-a-lifetime burial yard for things.

And so, I remodel cemeteries, scrub out names, surnames, sorrow, birth and death dates, they are dumb-mouthed, an egalitarian cemetery. Put flowers on Jānis' grave, Pēteris', Andersons', Smelovs'. I let flower bearers know it doesn't matter, any grave will do in this cemetery purged of personality, where eye to eye with death, zero is zero. See, blank head stones.

You there, chisel words – those he picked up, suffered, unhappy and happy, but only those of his table of commandments. Musical notations, perhaps. Formulae perhaps. Student signatures, perhaps two or three out of a hundred, whatever. Cut his character's code into stone. The equation of his soul. You don't know it? Then why bring flowers? Because it's the thing to do? A habit? Duty? Then write on the cross: "He drilled duty into me for duty's sake" – or: "He schooled me in the necessity of sham sincerity."

But maybe his epitaph lies in his last will, convinced you never understood his life, could never crack the equation to his CREDO. Not in his will either? Disposable assets, yes, the soul's disposition, no? Then I don't know. At least consider what you'd write in your own will, or on your own stone. It could happen, after all, in 50 years, as your hour draws near, there'll be a sociological sub-section – epitaphology – the study of your documented life: socio-ethical values decipherable in your tombstone script – and whether you deserve burial in a cemetery, in this enormous bibliographical bastion, or back behind the dam, as soulless pagans were. Let eternal peace and eternal life be granted unto you, as you are now granted a company or government pension, only you'll have to prove that subsequent generations will want to bother about what's written on your stone.

Wife, I understand you, he was your husband. That is his life's only justification. You loved him, he loved you but your love's short of witnesses, you have no children (and even so, children seldom prove love). I know, you can't cut his thrilling touch, his caring for your days, into cold stone – it's all slipped through your fingers, disappeared, unprovable. But maybe you're mirrored in the black stone – clear-eyed youth to the despair of his dying day in your cheeks. Nothing's more precious than love – not astronomy or atomic physics – the legacy least susceptible to encoded details. Signless. Too big for signs.

Write simply, truthfully. If he was a crook, don't cover up. He had his own truth, crucial for others to know, constructing their own.

Be frank:
– He never settled his debts.
– He had more children than his wife bore.
– She never squeezed toothpaste tubes at the end but in the middle, he ladled sour cream from the centre of the bowl, her life neither ripe nor rotten.

That too evokes a personality. This, a pithy precis of life.

Epiphany XII

Head stroking. Stroking memory. We are stroked. When we were small. So we recall. Simple stroking of a child's head, fingers threading the hair. Pet, whisper a pet name. No regrets. So simple.

But stroke a silver head. Grandmother, grandfather, uncle when he's sick. And he'll begin to cry. Confused, he'll begin to cry. About what?

There was fire there once. Constant fire close by and reflections flaring full of promise. There was always warmth behind the wall, and sometimes it seeped under the door.

Stroking – stroking memory.

So – it's hard to stroke a silver head. No fondling hand settles a debt with a nickel.

Kleptomania

steal from your mother and
store with your wife
steal from your wife and
store with yourself
steal from yourself and
store in a poem
steal from a poem and
store within
and stymied without storage
steal from within.

Autumn Leaves In Latvia

> *Over racks of amber barley*
> *Evening's copper bell has come.*
> *What you mean to me*
> *Is beyond words, and then some.*
>   FOLK SONG

Autumn leaves in Latvia, a pod splits its seams,
    cabbages are plump.
Heat lightning, musk of plums, and Valdemārpils
    seed my dreams.
Autumn leaves in Latvia, and sad cicadas chirr
    in the still dusk.
Like a horse, it seems, led into the fields,
    safe again from killer wolves.
Blessed with time to tumble through the fog
    and softly whinny in the moonlight,
I wait for someone with a sugar cube,
    a stroking hand.

White mist clings to the fields,
    what's the fog busy hiding?
A blood moon! Firs funnelled in darkness.
    Brethren ride to war.
Strangers whisk the orphan girl away unseen
    through the farflung night,
Laima marking her trail,
    as conjurers cast spells...

And night black as a dog, glossy autumn dew,
    and grasshoppers stand still.
A star nicks heaven, a will-o'-the-wisp marshlight
And chilled to the bone.

I fall asleep
    as another star peeps over the lean-to.
No one around knows infinity terrifies me.
A lush land! Why do I feel
    paltry and poor?
And euphoric in the moonlight, nicotine petals
    snicker at me

Yearning As the Dove

pondskin
sacred and green
as a sunlit frog's
evening sheen

pick an apple
pluck a stone
they spell a tale
of landhome

the lark
skies so far
from mice in the stubble
piglets in a jar

mother   bond
so close   quiescent
green and laden
and bent

alone at the evening
sauna, my love
for friends yearning
as the dove

Epiphany XIII

Enough, I've had it with teaching the world! Someone must be left unschooled. A dog beside me, a red tongue!

A dog with a red tongue scatters my tulips, refuses to heel – an unschooled dog!

Will I ever again crow in the dark like a rooster, clap ears like an alarm clock?

While hundreds chase the streetcar, let Her sleep! Sleep if She wants! Doze at Her work at the dispatcher's desk. Lie down, slender pole of mercury in the thermometer. The overheated sun melts, mercury lies dead-still.

Let Her sleep at hockey games, in racing cars! Let Her sleep in the starting blocks and the barrels of starting pistols.

And dance where dancing is disdained! A tarantula on the payroll sheets! She dances on the chart, and knocks her knees on the digits. Such splendid legs! I'm awfully sorry She banged her knees on the numbers!

The sleeping cap settles over us, moon slightly askew, like a worn-out slipper. Peace of the nightgown covers the earth – only the weasel noses among stars! Because she is unschooled. She wakens at night and eats, nibbling at the stars as if they were jam-jars.

Bear one unschooled child! May he know nothing of the clock. The world is a huge clock's dial, the hand herding the crowd along. The hand's a spade, a shovel. Flees the hand, it's a scythe, the crowd races around the dial.

Some run with the minute hand, some the second, as others shuffle after the hour hand. Whatever your timing, time is time. Whichever your hand – it's just style. A sprinter by nature, you'll run with the second hand. A marathoner, the minute hand's your man. But if you track the hour hand, – no matter, nothing's lost.

Forge ahead of the hand, harried and frightened, or lag behind, keeping close, – it's also a matter of style. Sprinters are short of time, snatching buttered bread off the table in the morning, and as the minute hand wheels around, you flee – the hand sweeping over the table, the table static – on the other side. You forget your mittens at home, but don't go back – that's where the swooping hand comes from.

Dear hearts, the hand swoops again – no time! – you snatch your children, can't count them in time, whether you've got them all (and you don't) – no time! no time! – the sweeping hand, and Kārlītis lags behind the hand and who knows how he'll end up!

It's easy spotting people who feel the hand on their back. They run with one shoe on, the other off. Women with smeared lipstick – finding the hand on their back in the mirror, frightened to death, they've drawn a quick line, crooked and garish. Up and out, down the street.

A torn stocking, unshaven, unpressed pants, unclean teeth, an unshod horse and soft tires – so we take off, no time to pause. And behind us, like a shepherd with his crook, the hand herding.

We, the others, all queue behind the hand. As insurance, we know we've a spare sweep of the hand. We try not to fall behind, and if a shoe slips off, we can still pick it up, step into it. We've time to spare – sew a button, shine shoes, love up the wife a little, nail Jesus to the cross. We've time to spare, catch up to the hand, eager not to fall too far behind. We say: don't fall behind the times.

But someone sleeps. Curls up on the dial, indifferent. I want to school him, scream, the hand will lop his head, chop his arms, you've got to keep up with the times, that…But nothing happens. The hand sweeps over him, he slumbers. I wait wide-eyed, wondering when he'll lift his head. Yes, wakening, but as the hand passes, he bends to sniff a flower. The hand's coming, he pokes around for bee honey, hunkers down to sip at the spring. Calmly cleans his shoes. Just as the judicial hand comes, some small thing happens – on his knees, he digs potatoes in a drill or loses his knife in the grass, or lets the pail drop into a well and crawls in after it. The hand sweeps overhead, harmless. A coincidence? He lives, as if time hardly mattered.

I wanted to school him. Still, someone should be left unschooled.

Blues

Butterflies in the blue, blueflies, blue sky's bluebirds
whiten softly
soften white
falling fall

snow-bound woods snow boughs bury us

long gone
a goner long gone
we'll have to live
white partridge scurries unsleeping white mole tunnels

white rooster crows
a white song
sinking into snow
spruce twigs' white fir cones rustle

the white chains of
alert white dogs, their
teeth chattering

like ruffled sparrows we'll share cold

long gone
a goner long gone
it'll snow

Knit Long Stockings

> *White wool, girls, spin white wool*
> *we'll knit long stockings;*
> *until the ancient Mother of Cows returns*
> *breaking white ice.*
> FOLK SONG

girls, knit long stockings
for the nones of winter
a hand darting into the blouse
the nones of loneliness

Pēteris of the warm hands
Juris the warmer
none touch you now
now none come

aie, Madara, a climbing madder
falls as youth fades,
Mārtiņš weeps for his chrysanthemum,
autumn's rose

a lone red cranberry
neither whines nor whispers
since the cranes have flown,
but is still poised in case a crane...

Pēteris of the warm hands
Jānis the warmer
none come now
now the nones of winter
girls, knit long stockings
as high as high can be

The White Fairy Tale

Virgin snow fell last night. Now the world is white. So white it's a whiteout. The white hen laid a white egg, losing it in the snow. The white rooster's white song flew under the eaves and froze, a hanging icicle. The white squirrel had white little squirrels who leapt onto white branches, and the squirrel couldn't find them any more. A blizzard of trees – a white tree lost in a white day in the woods.

A twirl of white chimney smoke, and even ink in the bottle is white – I don't know whether you'll be able to read what I've written. We eat only white bread, drink white coffee. This morning I cleaned my boots – with white polish!

Gauja is white – I threw in a line, reeled in a white pike and found a white duckling – alive in the stomach (swallowed by the glutton!), so I clipped this note to the duckling's tail feathers, let her go, and she flew off. If she finds you, feed her, trim her wings (so she won't fly away), and every evening warm her tummy with a white water bottle. Write me if she lays a golden egg!

At Maruža's

> *Give Mārina that wee cow,*
> *left as the last of a hundred.*
> FOLK SONG

when your wee cows
are none, every one,
take that little cow
left as the last of a hundred

strain, strain,
the residue
draining from the milk pail
left as the last of a hundred

pare, pare,
penny flute pare
play that penny song
left as the last of a hundred

battles done, to come
as I cut and run
undercover
left as the last of a hundred

all, all burned to the ground
a small child in the scorched shell
child
left as the last of a hundred

It Was A Beautiful Summer

It was a beautiful summer.
We were wily as flowers.

In May we were wily as dandelions
and words dandled behind us like bees
with pollen in their pockets,
yellow.

Painless, talking as catmint.
Painful talking as lilacs –
the lilac nights of burned out words
whose ashes lie in the heart.

In July we were wily as poppies
with words enclosed in their buds.
Now, with no one watching,
I rattle the poppy pods –
it's how I talk to you
alone.

Then we were wily as nettles
and prattled on and on as nettles.
Too much, perhaps.
I suppose we should have kept our peace
as nettles.

Because, in autumn
when we were wily as gladioli,
one as common pink,
the other – as carmine,
we were completely confused.

Still later, the aster
colors clashed.
Your words were mauve,
mine yellow,
and I never heard a word.

Then it all withered.
Only immortelles were left.
Yesterday I put up the storm windows
and immortelles are in bloom
between the panes.

I sit alone by the window,
musing to myself
as an immortelle
Saying:
"Soon frost will appear on the panes
as flowers of ice.
As such, I refuse to say
another word."

Epiphany XIV

What's doing, death you old Roman candle!

All burns to a crisp. Grandmother burns, her dahlias burn.

I lope along the furrow, astride shoots, yanking carrots from the drill. I'm a small boy. I steal carrots but before I can haul them over the fence my carrots crisp like Roman candles.

Sitting here in my room. All's burning, spitting sparks. Your photograph's a sequined flame. The burning ruler sheds centimetres as ash at one end. The telephone burns like a Roman candle, our chat, so short. I say "thank you" and "goodbye" – words burn, glittering.

What's this, midnight sun, the room's aglow with sparks? Every last thing I've culled and coveted burns to a glittering crisp. Meaning what? Am I now a lowly beggar going to beg? But light suffuses the room, and I am suffused in light, and maybe even the heart burns to a glittering crisp.

I still intend to say something, but whatever I say burns like a Roman candle. And this is the final sentence – "The heart burns, glittering."

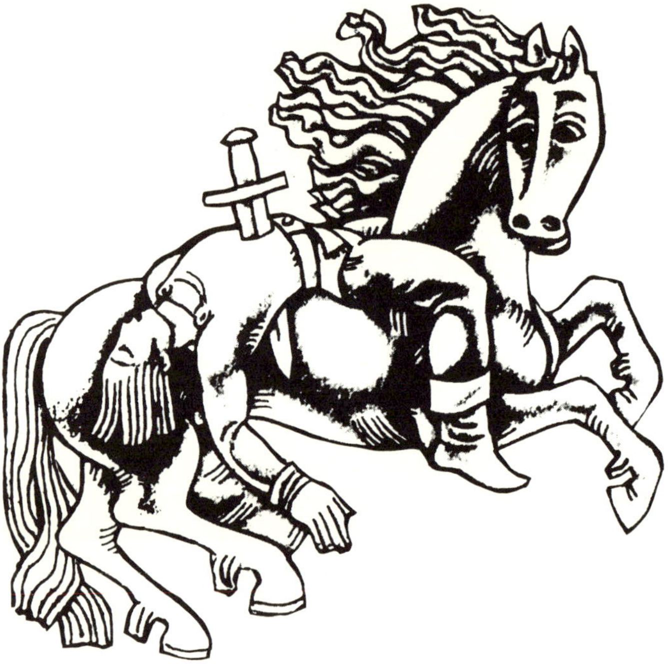

Translator's Notes

The ancient Latvians came from lands southeast of the Tigris-Euphrates basin. Their language, therefore, has roots in Sanskirt. But by 2000 B.C. they had migrated north, settling near the shores of the Baltic Sea. They were an agricultural people who cleared farms between swamps and forests.

They believed in God, *Dievs*, who – for all his sacred and profound powers – was more a wise counsellor and helpmeet in human affairs than a stern law-giving lord; *Māra*, also known as *Zemes māte* (Mother Earth) – who is much like the Celtic triple goddess – the giver of life, the young woman sacred among trees, springs and rocks, and as *Veļu māte*, the Old Crone, the layer-out of the dead; and *Laima* the power of fate – who operates loosely between *Dievs* and *Māra*. Also venerated were *Pērkons* (Thunder), *Saule* (the Sun, who is feminine), *Jumis* (eternal or recurring life) and nature spirits like the Sea Mother, the Forest Mother, and the Wind Mother. Evil is embodied in *Velns* or *Jods* (the Devil) and his human helpers – sorcerers and witches. There is no equivalent to the Christian Fall or doctrine of original sin, no shame at the flesh or sense of sin. A modernized version of this ancient religion, popular since Latvia's brief time of independence, 1918 – 1940, is called *Dievturība*.

Over the centuries, the Latvian farming clans built up a huge corpus of songs. These folksongs are called *dainas*. They do not have an integrated narrative structure, but are filled with commentary on *Dievs, Laima* and *Māra*, rituals, daily life, communal celebrations and calendars of the universe. Song is the tie that has bound. When Ziedonis, in "By the Roadside" scribbles a song with an old coal on ruined chimneys as apple trees and hops take root, he is touching on the sense of perpetual renewal that runs through the *dainas*, a renewal that is necessary after 800 years of occupation and re-occupation by one army or another. In fact, most of Ziedonis' poems contain echoes, images, and sometimes lines from the ancient songs, and he has had a huge lot of songs to live with. The definitive collection of *Latvju dainas* compiled by the legendary Krišjānis Barons around the turn of the century contains 35,789 songs, accompanied by clusters of variants – some 182,000 additional texts. Most of these are quatrains, but some ten percent are long songs. The entire corpus contains almost one million lines, the largest single repository of published oral folklore in the world. By this time, the collection in the archive has grown to more than one million *dainas* and variants.

They are cast in the metrical mold of a rigorous double symmetry – the first two lines usually deal with an image from nature, the last two with an analogue from human affairs. Each song, therefore, is a self-contained epigram or poem. Arranged thematically in cycles and sequences, they form an ancient cosmogony, a mythology and sense of social order, and take on a scope that is epic in feel if not in structure. The lyrical "I" of the songs is not an individual's voice but the voice of the people, singing in an eternal present of different lives all following the same archetypal pattern. The *dainas* are not about a specific Līze, Made, Mikus, or Pēteris, but about the Bride, the Bridegroom, the Mother in all her selves, the Brothers and the cleavages between clansmen. Ziedonis' ladies – Apars, Marta, Alīna, and Annele – should be read this way.

This world is held together by Cycles of Eternal Return (circles of stones, geometric circles) that spiral around the Sun and lesser astral bodies. The Sun is the cosmic clock, daily riding up the Hill of Heaven. Not surprisingly, the summer and winter solstices and the spring and fall equinoxes are the spokes in the early wheel of Time. Various communal celebrations attend to these moments in Time, birth, growth, death – followed by an endlessly repeating cycle of creation, increase, and destruction. This is the framework for religious beliefs, ethical values, the social order. This the framework for the metaphysics of the *dainas* – in which the aim of life is to live in harmony with the gods, nature rhythms, and fellow clansmen. This is the framework for Ziedonis, citizen of contemporary Riga in contemporary Latvia.

The Epiphanies. Ziedonis has published several collections of prose poems, or "epiphanies." He sees them as "little stimuli, little flarings up," and such "apparitions" are part of his "attack on the habitual," his anger at any imposition of the ordinary. "Our poetry," he says, "should defend the individual. Poets represent the spiritual culture of Latvia, and it is poetry that is the defender of individuals. At the same time, poetry must, in purely tactical terms, always find itself close to the borderline. Poetry must find itself close to the boundaries, close to all boundaries, because only there is poetry born. That is my conviction. Therefore, poets find themselves in exposed places. Where border guards are, there are also poets. That's our poetic struggle here. We must also awaken the ethical values of the Latvian folk song. Because with all the historical events we have lived through, we have acquired new values and new beliefs. Somewhere, perhaps, we have lost a link, but we have not distanced ourselves so far that we cannot find the link again. I do what I can. That is all."

In seeking that link, Ziedonis shares in certain aspects of the ancient *dainas*. Neither the songs nor Ziedonis talk about gods or the powers that control the world, but to them, with a belief in the force of the word to defeat evil, whether it's the devil or a prince. This is an animistic world, *dievota*, as it is put in one *daina*, i.e. infused with the divine spirit (hence the veneration of an endless number of "Mothers"), but also – in many songs – there is a sense of personal insight that is very close to the Greek idea of illumination, or epiphany. Ziedonis has the best of both worlds: a moment of individual revelation that is, in its resonance, communal.

In the Latvian tradition, the moment of epiphany is often linked to trees (reminiscent, again, of the ancient Celtic intimacy with trees, for their alphabet, as sacred groves, and the tree-tops – wherein the poets leapt across the land), and we must remember that in this animistic world everything – every bird, flower, stone – is alive with significance. The word "white," for example, has almost as many meanings for the Latvian as the word "snow" for the Inuit. In this first Epiphany, thrushes are close to the birch, storks to the oak, there is the scent of sacrificial wood smoke, and elsewhere in songs, *Māra* sits in a willow, *Laima* in a linden, *Pērkons* in an oak.

At Maruža's. The divine power as wife or mother is *Māra*. She is invoked during a woman's labor. Magic incantations are used as children enter the world "through the gates of *Māra.*" She, like other such figures, is closely linked with totemic animals: cows, particularly black cows spotted with white; a black beetle, a black hen, a black toad, a black snake. According to the chronicles, the ancient Latvians kept tame snakes in their houses, feeding them dishes of milk (such tame snakes also occur in the cult of the Great

Goddess in Crete). Milk is mother's nurturance at the beginning of life and the cow's, the sustaining sustenance in the social order. As for the "grim German monks" with their "code of cleanliness," they arrived on the shores of the river Daugava in the 12th century. The main armada, twenty-three ships of crusaders led by Bishop Albert of Bremen, conquered the five Latvian peoples (Livs, Cours, Semigallians, Letgallians and Sels). This was the beginning of the Christian incursion and 800 years of conquest and occupation.

Krišjānis Peters Was Just Born. Midsummer night is an ancient orgiastic feast celebrating the summer solstice. It is on the 24th of June, now known in many countries as the feast day of John the Baptist. In Latvia, it is called *Jāņi* (Johns), and *Jānis –* known as *Dieva dēls* – God's son (who has nothing in common with the Christian Son of God) he has functions that are similar to those of the Greek, Dionysus – an archaic fertility god. The force he incarnates is Eros – not Eros, the puckish boy with his play-arrows – but the force that compels inorganic matter *and* male and female to come together. In him lies the generation and perpetuation of biological life.

The summer solstice is the moment in the solar year when light defeats darkness, and it is the moment of cosmic transition (the Sun hangs in the balance on its upward/downward journey) when the barriers between men and gods collapse, a twilight moment of magic when bridled and unbridled force are on the loose. *Jānis* rides the whole year, arriving on Midsummer night to see whether the crops have been good and whether his name is being celebrated. At the centre of the Latvian celebrations is a ritualistic communal meal. Along with singing and foods – especially cheese and beer – and garlands of oak leaves and flowers, fire plays an important part in the idea of continuous and perpetuating life. Buckets of burning pitch are hoisted atop tall poles placed on hills, the fires echoing each other. Bonfires are also kept burning through the night, and linking fire with the vegetable world is the mythical fern, which – *dainas* suggest – blossoms once a year, only on Midsummer night. Its possession brings mystical powers, luck, prosperity.

Tree. In this poem about the uprooting of peoples, there is an unsolvable translation problem. The tree that is rooted into the earth in Latvian is the *ieva*, which is a kind of choke-cherry tree that also suggests *Ieva*, or Eve in the garden of Eden. I have settled on the linden, which has its own connotations: it is female and associated with fertility, but obviously, a potent word play is lost.

Lāčplēsis (Bearslayer) is an epic poem in six cantos by Andrejs Pumpurs. It appeared in 1888. Pumpurs' sources were "a few Latvian folk legends," but his hero *Lāčplēsis* and his companion *Koknesis* (Bearer of trees) have seized the Latvian psyche. Bearslayer was a foundling, suckling at the breast of a she-bear, found in a sacred grove. A tribal chief raised him as a son, and he became a noble storybook leader of a people who had in fact – through the 12th and 13th centuries – lost their lands to German invaders. Bearslayer's heroism has an obvious national appeal: total dedication to defeating giants and monsters and so reunifying the people; but he also has another task, to enter the sunken castle of Burtnieki, the place where sacred scrolls are hidden. Bearslayer is not only to free the conquered lands (during its twenty years of independence, the Latvian republic called its highest military decoration the Order of Lāčplēsis) but he is also to act as a culture hero, restoring the collective memory, making sure the people do not forget their *dainas*, their lore, their cultural bonds and ethics.

Epiphany III. Lielupe is a river in Latvia.

Love Was So Mute. There is no such word in English as "inostensible" but there ought to be because the meaning is clear, so now there is.

Handlebars. This poem is from the "Motorcycle," one of Ziedonis' first books. Published in 1965, it caused a sensation in Latvia and among poets in the Soviet Union. The poem, "By The Roadside," is from this collection as well, and one of the dominant themes is obviously travel and the freedom of the road.

The Poem Began. "In, with, and under / Christ's blood" are the exact words used in the Lutheran liturgy.

Latvia, O Butter Churn. The effect of this poem on audiences in Riga, when it is read to them, cannot be conveyed on the page. It is ironic in its opening and provokes laughter: at present the butter churn is not bursting at the seams. The stanza beginning, "O Marta! The city's forgotten our folk songs," speaks to the loss of cultural memory that threatens the people, so the poem rather than being a celebration – as it at first seems –is a lament, ironic and pleading.

Trio. "She leaves behind / replete rye / and weeping cornflowers." This is just one of many times when something growing – in this case, rye – is associated with a particular sex, rye being male.

Autumn Leaves in Latvia. Valdemārpils is a small town in Latvia named in honor of Krišjānis Valdemārs, a prominent Latvian national figure.

The White Fairy Tale. Gauja is a river in Latvia. Some of the most romantic contemporary songs have been written about this river.

By The Roadside. "Luck poured / into the tureen on New Year's Eve." On New Year's Eve, lead was melted to a liquid state and then poured into water. The shape that formed instantly was taken out of the water and held against candlelight. The shadows on a wall were interpreted for the future.

To understand how indebted I am for insights into the *daina* tradition and Latvian mythology to Vaira Vīķe-Freiberga, professor at the University of Montréal, interested readers need only consult these essays: "The Lyrical and the Epical in Latvian and Finnish Folk Poetry," *Journal of Baltic Studies*, 1987; "The Major Gods and Goddesses of Ancient Latvian Mythology," B. Kangere, H. Rinholm. *Festschrift for V. Rūķe-Draviņa*, Stockholm, 1987; and "Andrejs Pumpurs's Lāčplēsis ('Bearslayer'): Latvian National Epic or Romantic Literary Creation?" *Acta Universitatis Stockholmiensis – Studia Baltica Stockholmiensa* 2, 1985.

And finally, I should explain that I neither read nor speak Latvian. I was given working translations by Baņuta and Baiba Rubess. They quite deliberately did not seek felicity of phrase; they sought accuracy of meaning, no matter how awkwardly stated. I studied these for days, weeks, sometimes months, trying over two years to get hold of the inside of the poem, trying to feel the meaning and think the music, seeking an equivalent to the original. This is an act of faith, and hope. Once I arrived at my own versions, I consulted with several Latvians who know Ziedonis' work intimately. This was an act of trust. I am told these versions approach the original; that Ziedonis has a voice in English. I hope so. I have inhabited for a moment the mind of a man I've never met, and want to be fair to him.